PITTSBURGH PRAYS

THIRTY-SIX HOUSES OF WORSHIP

ABBY MENDELSON
TIM FABIAN
BRIAN COHEN

THREE BLIND MICE PRESS

"Pittsburgh Prays
Thirty-Six Houses of Worship"
copyright © 2012 Abby Mendelson, Tim Fabian and Brian Cohen
Three Blind Mice Press

On the cover: First United Methodist Church, Shadyside.

This book is for our children

Acknowledgements

Any book -- especially one with three names on the cover -- is by necessity a collaboration, and as the writer in the family I am indebted to many people without whom *Pittsburgh Prays* would not have come to life.

Tim Fabian, whose extraordinary images illuminate both *The Steps of Pittsburgh* and *The Bridges of Pittsburgh*, conceived of this book, then asked me to join him. We went to two churches; he shot, I scribbled, and it remains an honor.

When Tim's life skittered in a different direction, he asked Brian Cohen to continue the project. Brian, with whom I have worked on many other assignments, was my other, better half. Aside from creating this book's remarkable look, Brian, while shooting assiduously, accompanied me on all the interviews. He listened carefully, then asked the telling question that I had managed to omit. He invariably added depth and richness, and the text often reflects his thinking as much as it does mine.

Cheryl Towers and Harold Maguire, who had previously published books by Tim and me, encouraged us from the outset. Without them, *Pittsburgh Prays* would not exist.

In the beginning, to help clarify my thinking, I sent out the inevitable battery of e-queries. Dear friends Adrienne Block, Bob DeFazio, Peter Oresick, Mary Ann Pike, Renee Rosensteel, and Michael Simms were incredibly helpful, pointing me in right directions, steering me away from dead ends. Fine scribes, as well as good friends, including the late Walter Kidney, Rick Sebak, and Frank Toker, also blazed a trail for us.

Without the myriad volunteers and clergy -- far too many to list here -- who opened their buildings for us, then gave us tours, coffee, and countless hours sharing their stories, this book would be little more than notes cribbed from the 'net.

Nor would it be anything without the endless patience, staunch support, and boundless enthusiasm of our wives, Judy Mendelson, Karen Fabian, and Ilyssa Manspeizer, without whom we could accomplish nothing.

Finally, in this life we never know what impact a house of worship might have. When I was 17, the University of Pittsburgh sent a recruiter to my Long Island high school. Intrigued, my late mother and I came for a look-see -- my sole college visit. Taking a tour of the campus, we were suitably impressed -- until we hit Heinz Chapel. Soaring, majestic, it literally took my mother's breath away. It was Heinz Chapel that sold Pitt -- and Pittsburgh -- to her. (I thought it was swell, too.) I came here a callow 18-year-old -- and received a world-class education, married, raised a family, created a career, and never left.

Thank you, Mr. Heinz, for all you've done for me.

A.M.

TABLE OF CONTENTS

    Acknowledgments 1

    Introduction 5

1. St. Mary of Mercy, Downtown 9
2. Beulah Presbyterian Church 13
3. First Presbyterian Church 19
4. Emmanuel Episcopal Church 24
5. St. John the Baptist Ukrainian Catholic Church 29
6. Immaculate Heart of Mary Church 33
7. Muslim Community Center of Greater Pittsburgh 38
8. St. Louise de Marillac Church 42
9. First Hungarian Reformed Church of Homestead 47
10. Temple Emanuel of South Hills 52
11. Pittsburgh New Church 57
12. Sri Venkateswara Temple 63
13. Zen Center of Pittsburgh 67
14. Old St. Patrick's Church 70
15. Pittsburgh Sikh Gurdwara 75
16. St. Nicholas of Myra Byzantine Catholic Chapel 79
17. St. Anthony's Chapel 85
18. St. Nicholas Croatian Catholic Church 90
19. Macedonia Church of Pittsburgh 94
20. St. Nicholas Orthodox Church 100
21. Rodef Shalom Congregation 104
22. St. Paul Cathedral 108

23.	EAST LIBERTY PRESBYTERIAN CHURCH	112
24.	HEINZ MEMORIAL CHAPEL	118
25.	HINDU JAIN TEMPLE	122
26.	THE PRESBYTERIAN CHURCH OF SEWICKLEY	127
27.	CALVARY UNITED METHODIST CHURCH	131
28.	ST. BENEDICT THE MOOR CHURCH	135
29.	ST. STANISLAUS KOSTKA CHURCH	139
30.	ST. MARY OF THE MOUNT CHURCH	144
31.	FIRST UNITED METHODIST CHURCH	148
32.	CONGREGATION POALE ZEDECK	154
33.	SMITHFIELD UNITED CHURCH OF CHRIST	159
34.	ST. AUGUSTINE CHURCH	164
35.	ST. JOHN CHRYSOSTOM BYZANTINE CATHOLIC CHURCH	169
36.	TRINITY CATHEDRAL	173
	Addresses and Locations	180
	Photo credits.	181

INTRODUCTION

Pittsburgh Prays: Thirty-Six Houses of Worship

Experienced Pittsburghers, we could hardly miss the extraordinary buildings that populate the landscape. In every neighborhood, in every town, there were invariably several houses of worship, each with its own style, each with its own stories. On the way to doing other things, we all overlooked the treasures before us -- until we didn't.

As we thought through creating this book, we settled on criteria: stories, setting, style, stunning interiors. Each, we agreed, had to be different. Each had to be worthy in and of itself.

Of course, while any list is by definition arbitrary and capricious, we tried to be less so. While diversity was important, we never entertained the idea of universality, either denominationally or geographically. (I'll trade you two Methodists for a Presbyterian and South Hills Byzantine to be named later.) We went where the stories and the images took us; no doubt we have omitted many worthy places. But by and large, if there was nary a shard of stained glass nor a significant story, we tended to pass it by. For example, when a friend suggested to one of us *his* church -- as many did -- a plain, country church from back in the proverbial day, another nipped the idea in the bud. "Simply old isn't enough," he sternly warned, and we listened.

Nevertheless, we did try to be more rather than less inclusive, to include grand gestures as well as intimate spaces, East Liberty Presbyterian to the Zen Temple, massive cathedrals to private chapels.

The populations varied greatly, too. Some, like Saint Louise de Marillac, are robust, literally bursting at the seams. Others, like Homestead's Hungarian Reformed, are hanging by a slender thread -- while all up and down Tenth Avenue many of her brethren, once 15 strong, are closed, boarded, up for sale. (For all ablutions, please call Our Lady of Howard Hanna.)

Similarly, we decided that the book would highlight not only sacred places, and piety, but also the love that created and maintains these houses of worships of all faiths, foci of communities and neighborhoods. More than bricks and mortar, each building represents the lexicon of Pittsburgh history – and generations dedicated to the greater good. Some gave millions; others, countless working families, literally saved pennies and nickels every week to pay for their prayer places. We found names like Heinz and Horne and Mellon; we also found no story more poignant than that of the woman of meager means, her name lost to history, who worked menial jobs to be able to dedicate the doors on her now-long-gone Hill District synagogue.

Miraculously, they were all built. Despite poverty, despite privations and real economic hardship, of the Depression and other hard times, numerous houses of worship rose on country roads and city streets. Saint Patrick. Saint Mary of Mercy. Saint John the Baptist. No matter how dark the night, the money always seemed to be there.

Another criterion was that each building still function as a house of worship. Although there are many stunning and storied defrocked churches and synagogues throughout the region, we drew the line at restaurants and hookah bars, open-stage theaters and buildings waiting for buyers. Scratched from the starting gate, for example, were such cashiered landmarks as the Oakland Tree of Life Synagogue, now the Pittsburgh Playhouse; the Lawrenceville Saint John the Baptist Church, now the Church Brew Works; East End's B'nai Israel Congregation, now the Urban League; the North Side's Saint Mary Church, now The Priory; the South Side's Saint Michael the Archangel Church, now Angel's Arms condominiums. And so on.

Moreover, as spirituality shifts from the Deity to *DEE*-fense, and Pittsburgh hosts a smaller, more secular population, departed are the days when entire populations sought solace in the worship of their choice. With shrinking congregations, flagging funds, and aging facilities, the fortunate mothballed houses of worship have been sold to the highest bidders. Others – too many others – simply had their doors locked and environs abandoned.

Some houses of worship, lovely but unloved, have been bulldozed into rubble.

A century ago, there were 24 separate, identifiable synagogues in the Hill District alone. Now there are none.

Still, Pittsburgh retains a resilient religious spirit; after all, it is a city that was created -- and continued -- by profoundly observant people.

Since only the strong survive, successful houses of worship do whatever it takes to bring people into the building. From boxing clubs to bingo, jazz bands to bowling nights, religious institutions often unite the social as well as the spiritual, the secular and the sacred, sacraments and Steeler Sundays. In this, they are community centers, welcoming people where they are.

These days, some come to slap the skins, bang the bongos; others are born, baptized, married, and buried all in the same place. Where once Gothic lines and representational stained glass were all the rage, now the light is more muted, the spaces more conducive to meditation. As the treasures, and thinking, of earlier times fade, in some places grand organs and packed choir lofts have given way to the single voice, the strummed guitar.

In many cases, social action – from feeding the homeless to hurricane relief -- has replaced more traditional covered-dish suppers.

Nevertheless, for all the changes, virtually all spiritual leaders say that they welcome this new era, one of greater religious tolerance. At a time of cooperation, and communication, one spiritual leader smiled as he told of a visit from a leader in a different faith community, what a hit the man was on a Sunday morning, that after the visitor's sermon his congregants actually applauded. Then the spiritual leader added ruefully, "they never do that for me."

Smithfield United's Reverend Douglas Patterson could have been speaking for many spiritual leaders when he said that his congregants come from all over, for that is certainly the trend. With certain limited exceptions, no longer are houses of worship neighborhood endeavors or limited to walk-ins. Currently, it is hardly uncommon for people to drive great distances to find the congregation that's right for them. So while regular church attendance is down across the board, it is arguable that what replaced quantity is quality -- that people today really want to go to this or that particular house of worship. There's virtually no luck about it, no stumbling into it, which everyone agrees is a healthy sign, an indication of vitality.

A last word. Throughout the course of the visits, and interviews, we were continually struck at how, if we changed one or two words in any given sentence, anything that pertained to one house of worship, or one religion, could easily pertain to any other. We found they were all virtually interchangeable. This idea amused us greatly when one church leader launched into an *ad hoc* critique of the seemingly endless intra-congregational squabbles which he faces. Shocked by how familiar all the fights were, I asked him if he was really the fellow who sits three rows behind me in my own synagogue.

We all laughed.

But we all knew better.

CHAPTER ONE

St. Mary of Mercy, Downtown

As we dig into the western religious roots of Pittsburgh, some things are lost in time. Although there were certainly Native American rites at the Three Rivers, performed by the Seneca, Shawnee, and others, the first western religious services may have occurred when Sieur de La Salle landed at the Point. Although such things are not known with surety, it is likely that the expeditionary force led by the former Jesuit included at least one priest, as was common with 17th-century French explorers. Therefore, let us say that the first area mass could have been celebrated in 1670, the year of his arrival.

As we fast-forward some six decades, we do know that the 1729 de Lery expedition included priests, as well as the 1749 Celoron de Blainville look-see. In the absence of anything more substantial, some believe that Father Bonnecamp, a mid-century Jesuit, celebrated the first mass.

But that is all speculation. We do know from written records that the French arrived *en masse* on the evening of April 16, 1754. The following morning their chaplain, Reverend Denys Baron, a Recollect Friar, celebrated mass -- arguably the region's first.

Regardless of who first said words and passed out wafers, shortly after arriving the French built a chapel -- The Assumption of the Blessed Virgin of the Beautiful River -- inside Fort Duquesne, a scant two blocks from the present site of Saint Mary of Mercy, which, using geographic proximity, claims its status as spiritual grandchild of Pittsburgh's first church.

For four years, the French celebrated mass in Fort Duquesne, until, political and military fortunes turning against them, they torched the place and abandoned it.

In marched the British, General John Forbes heading the column, renaming the place for Sir William Pitt, Earl of Chatham. Unlike the more edifice-minded French, neither the short-lived Forbes nor his successors built any churches. While Pittsburgh was a pious place, lay readers and circuit-riding, itinerant ministers led prayers and officiated at life-cycle events.

By this accounting, then, Pittsburgh's second church came to life in 1808, drawing breath as St. Patrick's in the Strip.

Six decades later, in 1868, a group of Irish immigrants living in the Point converted a small house into a chapel. Calling it Our Lady of Consolation, and seeing themselves as the spiritual heirs of the early French church, they quickly became Saint Mary of

Mercy. Universally called Saint Mary of the Point, in 1874 the Right Reverend Monsignor Andrew Arnold Lambing, LL.D., became the first Pastor.

No, neither the Monsignor nor his little church had any delusions of grandeur. That was for St Paul's Cathedral, then on Grant Street, Pittsburgh's Downtown church. By contrast, St. Mary's was the parish of the Irish poor, where Father Joseph Coffee's famous sermons were delivered not in English, the language of the imperialist aggressor, but in Gaelic.

With the building bursting out the doors, in February, 1876, St. Mary's plunked down a cool $12,975 to buy a pre-owned Methodist church at Second Avenue and Ferry Street (which became the Boulevard of the Allies and Stanwix Street). Within three years, St. Mary's boasted some 1,900 members, opened a religious school, ran multiple daily masses.

The parish grew apace -- so much so that by the 1920s, even running five masses on Sundays, and 10 on Holy Days of Obligation, the 850-seat building was unable to accommodate its own worshippers. One 1929 photo, in fact, shows supplicants, in hats, overcoats, and their Sunday best, mobbed at the sidewalk, unable to fit through the door.

Even with the Great Depression upon them, in 1935 the parish broke ground for what would become the current 1,300-seat church (with auxiliary space for 700 more.) With rough white plaster walls, arches, and a vaulted ceiling, St. Mary's has the aura of being in an underground grotto -- perhaps a sepulcher.

In the 1930s, the church thrived -- boasting six full-time priests, ably assisted by its lay leaders, the Ushers Club. As one vintage photo illustrates, Father Daniel Lawless, who served for 42 years, 1921-1963, is surrounded by 17 very proper men in vested suits and ties, holding their hats; there, front and center, sits a youngish David Lawrence, not yet Mayor, but nevertheless a power in the newly triumphant Democratic Party. (His own funeral, some 30 years hence, packed the house.)

Surviving floods (a crack in the floor is the sole reminder of the 1936 St. Patrick's Day deluge, which devastated the area), fires (a brutal 1946 conflagration gutted the adjacent Wabash Terminal and environs), and urban redevelopment (which in the 1940s and '50s gave Pittsburgh Gateway Center and Point State Park -- and stripped away St. Mary's indigenous neighborhood), St. Mary's has been nothing if not adaptable, expanding its ministry beyond the church's walls.

In the 1940s, for example, Father Lawless, along with Father Francis Rieke, went to so many area fires to bring coffee, offer consolation, administer the last rites, they came to be known as the fire priests. From 1943-45 alone, Father Rieke answered 110 calls.

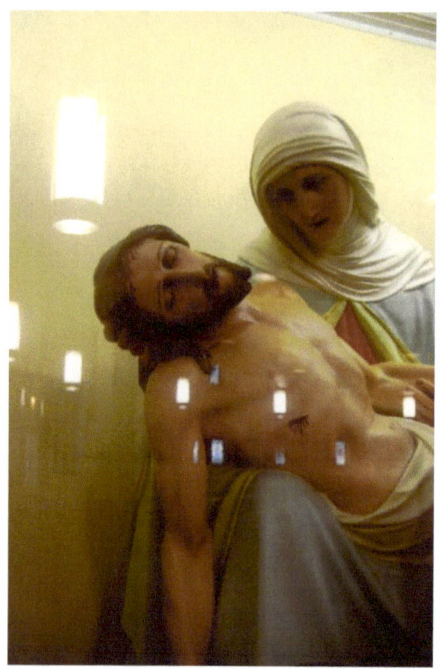

In the 1960s, the church held folk masses. A decade later, the church hired a social worker, offered alcohol counseling, opened a senior center. By '99, St. Mary's was also running a television ministry, the daily noon mass broadcast to some one million homes.

Although St. Mary's now has few registered parishioners -- at its nadir, it listed but three families as members -- the church nevertheless hosts hundreds of visitors weekly. While it's dropped from its zenith -- employing 11 full-time priests, running seven masses daily -- as John Cardinal Wright commented, St Mary's is "a center of devotion and a spiritual oasis in the Downtown area for the thousands who turn there for daily mass, devotional programs, and above all spiritual direction."

This is a role which the current pastor, Father Tom Sparacino, takes very seriously. "St. Mary's," he says, is "home to everybody – students, office workers, the homeless. It's a spiritual center.

"We're very much a transient parish," he adds. "At any given time in church, there are people of affluence. And sitting next to them are people from the street. One group is seeking respite from the pressures of life. The other is seeking respite from trying to stay alive."

Also known for the Red Door, on the Boulevard of the Allies, St. Mary's hands out some 100 daily bag lunches to the homeless. "A concern for the poor has been characteristic of the parish throughout its history," Father Sparacino says. "We help God's children wherever they may be."

In addition to feeding the homeless, Father Sparacino actively seeks them out -- and is so recognized around town that, aside from being constantly panhandled, he's often approached to hear confession right on the street.

A concomitant Walk-In Ministry offers groceries, clothes, blankets, and counseling to those in need. "People know that St. Mary's is here for a purpose," Father Sparacino adds, "to meet their spiritual needs." He pauses. "It's their home."

CHAPTER TWO

Beulah Presbyterian Church

In 1804, as Pitt Township Church's new minister James Graham rode west through Pennsylvania's verdant wilderness, he was struck by the area's incredible natural beauty, the rich, fertile landscape, the clean, rushing waters, the mountains teeming with game. With his new church there, what a perfect marriage, he thought, of the Book of Creation and the Book of Scripture. Considering the Hebrew word from *Isaiah, beulah*, married, Pastor Graham took as his text the Tenth Stage of John Bunyan's *Pilgrim's Progress*: "Now I saw in my dream that by this time the pilgrims were got over the Enchanted Ground, and entering into the country of Beulah, whose air was very sweet and pleasant; the way lying directly through it, they solaced themselves there for a season. Yea, here they heard continually the singing of birds, and saw every day the flowers appear in the earth, and heard the voice of the turtle in the land. In this country, the sun shineth night and day."

Christening his new posting Beulah Presbyterian Church, he did not live to see Pitt Township renamed for his church on the hill. Churchill.

Truth be told, as Pastor Graham would no doubt want it, he was something of a newbie at Beulah, for it had been sacred ground for decades before his ride across the mountains, even before the Republic. In 1758, as the British army headed west, there to engage the French at Fort Duquesne, they used the hilltop as a chapel in the fields, a wee dram of whiskey employed as an inducement to attract the troops. (No, Hamish, you reflect on the preaching first, *then* you take your ration.) On November 26, 1758, two days after the British conquest of Fort Duquesne, Chaplain Charles Beatty, a Presbyterian minister serving under General John Forbes, preached a Thanksgiving sermon at what was then called Bullock Pens.

For more than a half-century the settlers used a simple log cabin as their church, including the time, 18 years later, that they fought what the Anglicans derogatorily called the Presbyterian War -- for the many preachers who beat the Bible on Sundays, then hoisted muskets against the Crown and the Church of England on Mondays. That War for Independence was very real, and many were attracted by it -- and by the church where they heard the biblical preachings and the political broadsides, Revelations and Rebellion presented with equal valor and vigor.

George Washington himself was at Beulah, as were many others, including 33 Revolutionary War soldiers who gave their lives for the new Republic and are buried in the adjacent cemetery, one of them General John Johnston, Washington's own secretary. By 1813, the farmers who walked as far as 20 miles to church had outgrown their log cabin, replacing it with a wooden cruciform church, used for 24 years. Finally, in 1837, they built a church which still stands, the region's oldest continually used house of worship. Originally laid on logs, when the congregants saw that their simple rectangular church needed a sturdier foundation, they fired bricks right in the yard and re-set Beulah Presbyterian.

The beams hand-hewn, the window panes hand-made, Beulah was entirely devoid of ornament, a church far more about inspiring people's spirits than about imaginative figurations. Lovingly built and scrupulously maintained, it remains today what it has always been -- a simple farming church.

Over the years there have been distinguished visitors, of course, none greater than President John Tyler, who came, and sat, and whose chair remains unused to this day.

Unchanged for nearly a century, by the 1920s the congregation felt that it needed a basement -- which they proceeded to dig out of solid rock. Since then, they've added necessities only -- new carpets and pew cushions, window glass and light fixtures, a furnace to replace the old coal stove, even a sound system. Since the construction of a new church in 1957, the original version -- which they call the Chapel -- is used only for special holiday services, Ash Wednesday and Memorial Day, weddings, and occasional summer and evening services.

"The sense of history here is rather remarkable," comments Cynthia Reyes Fillmore, the current Pastor.

History, however, never stands still, and the new church building grew from a man as visionary as Pastor Graham. Coming in 1955, Pastor Dale Milligan -- "an aggressive, young, growth-oriented pastor," recalls church historian Bill Ritter -- invigorated Beulah Presbyterian Church. "Beulah is not a place of heavenly rest," the pastor said, charging his congregation to move ahead. "He had a way of getting people involved," church archivist Ruth Ann Ritter adds. "People couldn't say no to him."

Picking a site that once hosted the World War II Beulah Victory Garden, he challenged his flock. "Your dreams are too small," he thundered. "Build!"

Build they did, acquiring a full 10 acres adjacent to the old church, in 1957 completing the new church that stands today. Visible from the Parkway East, with a sanctuary

richly appointed in dark woods and abstract stained glass, it is a muted, moody space, simple yet deeply spiritual, giving rise to pensive, introspective prayer.

They built it -- and they came, Beulah becoming the happy recipient of what Bill Ritter remembers as "a lot of things happening at one time in one place." What was then called the Penn-Lincoln Parkway was completed, the post-World War II baby and building booms were at their collective height, and Westinghouse opened a major research facility right down the road. Suddenly, there was easy access -- and a lot of people. "This was literally a Westinghouse church in many people's minds," he adds.

In 1959 alone, Beulah welcomed nearly 700 new members -- swelling the ranks to the all-time zenith of some 1,900 people.

His work finished, Pastor Milligan left in early 1968, but the Beulah's mission has hardly abated. First, in what Ruth Ann Ritter recalls an "exciting time," the church started to reach out beyond its walls. Following what they had done a dozen years prior, when Beulah sponsored a Hungarian family fleeing the aftermath of the anti-Soviet revolt, they sponsored a Vietnamese family escaping the ravages of war. At the same time, they hosted exchanges with a Wilkinsburg-based African-American church. "That's pretty progressive for a Presbyterian church," Pastor Fillmore smiles.

That progressivism is the key to Beulah today. It's an old church, with a treasured history, but, comments Jim Behrenberg, the cemetery chairman who's in his eighth decade as a Beulah member "we don't live in the past. We *honor* the past. But we look to the future."

Today, Pastor Fillmore says, "there's a strong sense of calling to make a difference." For example, Beulah has adopted a sister church in Malawi, and has come to the aid of Katrina victims. "Beulah has lasted 225 years," she adds, "because it was always ready to re-make itself according to changing times and changing needs."

CHAPTER THREE

FIRST PRESBYTERIAN CHURCH

Every century brings its own changes and challenges. Facing the unknown, First Presbyterian Church had its own existential choice a century ago, as new technologies caused a crisis in the church.

Located on Sixth Avenue, Downtown, since the year before the Penn family sold the Reverend Samuel Barr two-and-a-half lots for five shillings in 1787, First Presbyterian watched as wood-frame houses gave way to steel-frame buildings, each equipped with high-rise elevators. Hemmed in by these new skyscrapers, challenged by skyrocketing Downtown real estate costs, the church's leaders realized that since it was no longer cost-effective to have single-family houses in the area, people who once walked to church were no longer in attendance.

The question arose: should the church follow its flock and relocate -- perhaps east, to Oakland, as did St. Paul Cathedral; perhaps west, to Sewickley, where so many of Pittsburgh's first families now resided?

Their answer was no, for they simply could not imagine Downtown without what they called Pittsburgh's First Church. Instead of departing, they decided to double their footprint, redouble their presence. "In 1900 it was radical when they decided to build this," gestures Reverend Thomas Hall, II, the current pastor -- and only the 15th since 1762, the year First Presbyterian was founded, lay ministers offering sermons in people's homes.

A decade later, Downtown's Presbyterian church hosted its first ordained clergy, Reverend David McClure and Reverend Levi Frisbie leaving New England to ride and, where necessary, walk some 700 miles to Pittsburgh. Straggling into town on August 19, 1772, mud-caked, flea-bitten, too sick to ride, they remained for some 10 months, preaching the gospel in the shadow of Fort Pitt -- and in small, *de facto* Presbyterian churches springing up around the area.

By August 1786, a year prior to buying the land from the Penn family, John Wilkins built a log cabin church on the current site. As membership grew, by 1805 they needed

a second building -- which they constructed of yellow brick around the small log church.

With services continuing unabated, they finished the outer shell, then simply dismantled the older, inner church, passing the logs through the windows and doors to be recycled elsewhere.

After the yellow brick church stood nearly a half-century, in 1853 they built a more substantial church, facing not Sixth Avenue but Wood Street.

Then technology bit, and as their decision loomed before them, in 1899 First Presbyterian hired Dr. Maitland Alexander, then of New York City's Harlem Presbyterian Church, to be its pastor. The very definition of the charismatic minister, Alexander was tall and robust, full of the right stuff -- what Pastor Hall calls "poise and power" -- to lead his church in the grandeur of Pittsburgh's Gilded Age, charged with making First Presbyterian "one of the great churches in the country," he adds.

Befriending the board for two-and-a-half years before starting his building campaign, by the time the pastor was ready for his revolutionary move, he had all the votes -- and support -- he needed. Laying the cornerstone in 1903, the new church was dedicated on Palm Sunday, April 16, 1905, "to the care of little children," he said, "and the comfort and consolation of the aged. We dedicate it as a refuge for all the storm-tossed, a shelter for the shelterless -- as a great rock for rest for the weary, and as a stream for refreshment for the thirsty."

When Pittsburgh meant power, and the Presbyterians were the proverbial top of the heap, such families as Craig, Laughlin, Herron, Dalzell, Chalfant, Denny, Speer, McKee, and Neville all participated in creating a magnificent space, a clear statement of the church's intent to maintain its historic stature Downtown. Facing Sixth Avenue, and the Duquesne Club, once the *de facto* seat of Pittsburgh power, they specified extensive, ornate carved sandstone and wood, along with 13 Tiffany windows, each 26 feet high and seven-and-a-half feet wide. With a 14th window coming from Charles and Frederick Lamb, there are also the massive Willet window facing the street, Clayton and Bell's visionary Stem of Jesse window in the rear of the chapel, and no fewer than 253 other stained- and leaded-glass windows throughout the church.

Unwittingly, perhaps, the church enjoys two unique aspects. First, the massive twin beams running the length of the church come from a single tree. Second, First Presbyterian's Tiffany windows were hand-painted on special-order Tiffany pastel cathedrals, then backed with Tiffany opalescent and Favrile glass. Afterward, it is said, Mr. Tiffany himself decided that he did not much care for the process and forever abandoned it -- making these 13 the world's only set.

All donated, of course, some windows cost as much as $3,000 each, a small fortune in turn-of-the-20th-century dollars. (Although the windows are literally priceless, they are insured for $2 million each today.)

"This," gestures Pastor Hall, "is their picture of what a church is supposed to be like."

His great church built, Pastor Alexander used it as Mr. Roosevelt did his Presidency, as a Bully Pulpit to rally Pittsburghers to the cause. During the First World War, for example, the pastor gave such stirring Noonday Talks to steelworkers, ship builders, and munitions fabricators -- whom he called Industrial Soldiers -- that they were frequently reprinted in the American and European press. "Our victories," went a frequent theme, "owe as much to the men who stand at the deck of the coke ovens, tap the holes of the blast furnaces, and turn the lathes of the machine shops as they do to the men at the front."

Never shy about sharing his pulpit, in 1914 Pastor Alexander gladly hosted the famous evangelist Billy Sunday -- as did his successors with Oral Roberts and Kathryn Kuhlman.

Maitland Alexander's service completed, he was succeeded by Clarence McCartney, a man with similarly outstanding credentials, including the imprimatur of William Jennings Bryan, three-time Presidential candidate, Secretary of State, and a pretty fair speaker himself. Serving from 1925-57, "McCartney was a rock star," Pastor Hall says. "What the Pastor said on Sunday made headlines the next day."

Living across the street at the Duquesne Club, he was so popular that church elders had to help him get through the admiring crowds on Sixth Avenue. Regularly drawing 1,600 worshippers on Sunday mornings, Pastor McCartney attracted 1,000 more at night. Founding the Tuesday Noon Club for Businessmen in 1930, an interdenominational group which met for lunch, song, and an inspirational message, he recruited more than 2,000 members, regularly drawing 800 and more.

McCartney's most memorable moment: preaching from the stone pulpit on Sixth Avenue, V.E. Day, May 8, 1945, to a Sixth Avenue packed with praiseful Pittsburghers.

This is again a new century, and there are again new challenges. Perhaps, as more people move back Downtown, there will be more regulars attending First Presbyterian. As it is, Pastor Hall says, "people drive by 20 churches to get here. They come in here and say, 'this is the most beautiful church I have ever seen.' They feel they're in the presence of an awesome and Holy God."

CHAPTER FOUR

Emmanuel Episcopal Church

Hands down, the North Side's Emmanuel Episcopal Church has the three best building stories in Pittsburgh ecclesiastical history. Now we're certain they're true. But if they aren't, well, as it says in *The Man Who Shot Liberty Valance*, "when the legend becomes fact, print the legend."

First, the architect. How did the good Episcopal folks in the City of Allegheny attract America's premier architect to design their replacement church, the original 1860s model having outlived its usefulness? Some believe that the rotund, idiosyncratic Henry Hobson Richardson pursued an unquenchable lust to design houses of worship. Hardly.

Sure, he had previously created four churches, but they were largely in his salad days. And sure, his North Congregational Church in Springfield, Massachusetts, in the style of an English country parish church, is something of a minor masterpiece. But by the 1880s Richardson sought grand civic projects – libraries, railway stations, metropolitan waterworks. In Albany, for example, he had designed the City Hall and State Capitol; in Pittsburgh, he salivated to get Allegheny County's Courthouse. A church? Maybe, but only one on a grand scale, Boston's Trinity, say. A teensy church in Allegheny? No way; it wasn't his dish of tea. And he wasn't the congregation's, either, this obese, obnoxious out-of-towner.

But there was only one vote in the room, and it was Malcolm Hay's. An influential board member and influential Grant Streeter, Hay knew that Richardson wanted the Courthouse -- but hadn't even made the short list. So Hay told Richardson, you do the Church, I'll get you the Courthouse.

Each man was as good as his word.

Typically grandiose, Richardson designed a $54,000 church – an eye-popping sum in the 1880s. Turnabout being fair play, the congregation allotted him a more modest $15,000. Swallowing hard, Richardson agreed do to the Lord's work. After some seven months, and 35 drawings, all parties agreed to the plans.

Second, the building. He may not have had a lot with which to work, but Richardson was nothing if not clever. Using good, working-class bricks -- hence the moniker the Bake Oven Church, for its simple facade -- plaster walls, and wooden beams, Richardson made Emmanuel Episcopal seem huge on a relatively small footprint.

Looking up at the bowed, beamed ceiling, one is immediately put in mind of an ocean-going vessel, and here's legend number two. It was, the dreamers say, another clever Richardson design feature, like the bowed walls, to make the building reminiscent of a ship's keel, with all its Christian overtones.

First, it's not a ship's keel, or at least wasn't planned that way. Truth was the highly rotund HHR liked to compose laying on his back. Whilst supine, watching his own ample girth rise and fall, he designed a version of it for the ceiling.

Second, the slate roof was so heavy it bowed out the walls -- Richardson never intended them to buckle. It is hardly a masterpiece of Richardsonian engineering; instead, it remains one of the Lord's miracles that the entire building hasn't collapsed under its own weight.

Third, the Gibson Girl. For the altar, Richardson wanted three stained glass windows and a simple wooden table. But with the Master gone -- he passed from Middle Earth shortly after the 1886 dedication -- the congregation was ready for finer trappings. First, in 1886, a $25,000 gift replaced the wooden table with a more imposing stone altar -- and added an organ. Five years later, in 1891, Mrs. William Thaw, Jr. -- from that Thaw family -- paid the princely sum of $75,000 to create a magnificent altar space as a memorial for her late husband. More or less directing the project herself, she commissioned art from the leading craftsmen of the day, including Leake & Green mosaics and Hunt and Tiffany stained glass windows.

Up in the balcony, which, accessbile only from outdoors, was originally reserved for servants, there are the Tiffany Alpha and Omega, Peacock (a symbol of the Resurrection), and so on.

At the altar there's a most lovely Hunt angel -- and therein lies a tale.

Taking his cue from the beauties of the day, Hunt followed the soft, flowing lines of the ethereal Gibson Girls. Created by famous turn-of-the-century illustrator Charles Dana Gibson, *les jeune-filles* resembled no one so much as his ace model -- Pittsburgh's own Evelyn Nesbitt. It could be; the resemblance is certainly strong enough to warrant the comparison.

Later in her infamous life, Ms. Nesbitt married Harry K. Thaw -- and was seriously, flagrantly unfaithful. Understandably enraged, Signor Thaw murdered architect Stanford White, one of his wife's special friends. Unforgiving, the Thaw family disowned Evelyn.

The delicious irony is that maybe -- just maybe -- she's the model for their stained glass angel. "I like to think there's some justice there," smiles the Reverend Donald Youse, Emmanuel Episcopal's current pastor.

Moving on. The carriage trade having long departed from Allegheny, Emmanuel Episcopal has evolved, as do houses of worship in neighborhoods and times that change.

Adding a boxing club, for example, in the more pugilistic 1940s, it hosted a motorcycle club in the free-wheelin' '60s. "Whatever it takes," Father Youse says, "to reach the neighborhood."

These days, he adds, the church "is a quiet beacon," attracting souls from all about the city. In many ways recapitulating Richardsons' original concept as an English country church, babies have been delivered there, people have taken refuge from floods, children have learned to read, down-and-outers have purchased cast-offs from the basement thrift shop.

Now reveling in a diversity that could barely have been imagined 130 years ago, Emmanuel Episcopal is a congregation that Father Youse calls "a bizarre mix of folk." Regularly ministering to upper middle class North Side gentrifiers and their neighbors who sleep under bridges, "we're 50-50 everything," he says, White/Black, young/old, name it. "It's not typical anything. It was never a planned deal."

Instead, he says, "it's been a place of healing for folks. People don't care who's reaching a hand to them."

Firebombed in the 1960s, when a Molotov cocktail crashed through a second-story window, a '90s foundation grant helped restore the sanctuary. "An impoverished parish always has an advantage," Father Youse says, adding that Emmanuel Episcopal never had the money to replace the Tiffany windows with more modern louver types, or to tear up the stunning yellow pine floor and lay down more up-to-date linoleum.

Conducting services which he calls Anglo-Bapist, a monthly highlight is the jazz service. Running second Sundays since the early '80s, the music draws a decidedly ecumenical crowd -- as well as such local luminaries as Etta Cox, Sandy Dowe, the legendary Lou Schreiber, Roger Humphries, and others. "There's a spirituality in jazz that's inherent and obvious," Father Youse says.

So is work in the streets. To rescue his flock, Father Youse has prayed in crack houses, challenged drug dealers, fought with police. "There are people with problems," he adds. "We're not going to cure hunger or homelessness. But we can walk with them."

"These kinds of challenges," Father Youse says, "allow me to wake up each day and say, 'Lord, I'm ready. What are we going to do today?'"

CHAPTER FIVE

St. John the Baptist Ukrainian Catholic Church

Arguably, it is Pittsburgh's most photographed church, because, posed properly, with the glittering Downtown offspring of Renaissances I & II behind it, the South Side's Saint John the Baptist Ukrainian Catholic Church, with its well preserved exotica -- the European-style golden domes, like bulbous onions, or peasants' noses -- sings of the city's blend of cultures, past and future.

Offering 19th Century versus 21st, there is also *kulturkampf* over ethnicity, about staying close and moving away, simultaneously escaping and embracing what was.

Those same polarities exist within the church as well. "The basic desire of all immigrant groups," offers St. John's bright, affable pastor, Father John Chirovsky, "is to preserve the past so you can address present and survive into the future" -- with all the tensions inherent thereof.

It's doubtful that Andrew Andreyszyn was thinking much about paradoxes, past and future, when he arrived in Pittsburgh in 1880.

Accounted as the city's first Ukrainian immigrant, he was followed almost immediately by Leon and Julian Wachnowsky. In less than a decade, the trio had been joined by 25 such families, all living on the South Side. Taking jobs in factories, mills, and mines, they prayed at the nearby St. Adalbert's Polish Catholic Church. Seeing the need for an Eastern mass, a priest came to celebrate the Byzantine rite in the adjacent school building. By 1889, the Byzantines were allowed to celebrate Easter in the church proper -- and it is said that they cried when they heard their own liturgy.

The following year, 1890, the Ukrainians had founded their own church and hired their first pastor, Reverend Gabriel Wyslocki, who stayed but a few months. Nevertheless, the fledgling congregation grew, and on September 1, 1891, spent $11,500 to purchase a frame hall from Grace Evangelical English Lutheran Church at Seventh and Carson Streets. In the 120 succeeding years, they've never moved from that corner, and in all likelihood never will.

Saint John's recorded its first baptism -- a girl named Anna Repacky -- on April 21, 1891. A century later, they had registered more than 9,000 more baptisms, accompanied by some 3,400 weddings.

In 1895, the Reverend Nicholas Stefanovich, from all accounts a dynamic leader who ably served the congregation for some 16 years, built a $75,000 brick church on the site (plus a rectory and a cemetery.) In 1915, Reverend Basil Merenkow arrived and initiated a campaign to enlarge building. When the adjacent row house burned down in 1917, "they took it as a sign from God," Father Chirovsky says, "and bought the property."

Thus grew the first community of Eastern Christians in Pittsburgh -- and those domes were an enormous draw. "People saw them," Father Chirovsky says, "and knew that was the place to go."

At first, Serbs, Ukrainians, Russians, and Poles all came to Saint John's. Then, gradually, they formed unique ethnic congregations of their own. Now, some 300 families still call Saint John Ukrainian their parish.

It's Byzantine, all right, the blue walls recalling heaven, the icon screen – but the Latinate stained glass windows? Locally designed and crafted, the windows were a sop to prove they were really Catholics, Father Chirovsky says. Pews -- not used in the traditional Orthodox rite (or in any Catholic church before the Reformation) -- were installed, a bow to America. "The melting pot theory," Father Chirovsky gestures, "was still prevalent."

With the exception of the domes, the architecture, too, is neither Ukrainian nor Byzantine. "Sometimes they nailed it," he shrugs. "Sometimes they were close, but no cigar."

For example, two panels which flank the altar enjoy some highly original artwork. On the right, artists tipped in some of the church's founders, including one man

who, after losing a leg in a smelting accident, somehow managed to donate $5,000 to Saint John the Baptist.

Along with the nameless benefactor there are church members dressed in garb that spans the decades, traditional Ukrainian dress to three-piece suits. Stage center, a decidedly Swedish-looking Christ, all blond hair and blue eyes.

On the left panel, Pope John XXIII and Pope Paul VI join with Ukrainian Bishop Soter Ortynsky, America's first.

"This church has gone through various stages," Father Chirvosky says, "like a human being growing up. It's interesting how things change through history."

The icon screen -- the third icon screen, Father Chirovsky points out, this one, in metal, more like an icon fence -- "invites people into heaven," he says. "It's not designed to keep people out, but instead an invitation to go beyond the world. And those that are in heaven are turned toward us and invite us to enter."

That is very Eastern; inside, however, there stands a baldachin, familiar to anyone who's seen Saint Peter's in Rome, four posts and a canopy. A Bernini knock-off, this one wound up on the South Side, Father Chirovsky says "because the congregation wanted to fit in."

But fitting in was hard, in the old days, inside the church and out. When an Eastern bishop came to Pittsburgh, for example, some Northern European clergy rejected his credentials out of hand: the man did not speak English, and was married.

The confusion was genuine. While Eastern churches have their own Patriarch and bishops, they are also Catholics aligned with Rome. (Officially, it is the Communion of the Patriarch and Church in Kyiv-Ukraine with the Pope and the Roman Church.) Having said that, the alliance has never been easy, and indeed dates back to the time when the capital of the Roman Empire was moved to Constantinople. As a new Eastern center of Christianity arose there, it evolved into the current Byzantine Church. And as the Byzantines, from Constantinople their missionary work, especially that of Saint Cyril and Saint Methodius, blanketed the Slavic peoples of Eastern Europe, establishing, among others, the very Church of Kyiv-Ukraine to which Saint John the Baptist swears fealty.

Although Saint John the Baptist has maintained that tie since its founding, the area has certainly changed over the years. For example, when the church was founded, the neighborhood was a sea of rowhouses -- meaning that parishioners stopped by for mass every day. Now, however, that the environs are decidedly mixed use, including Cupples Stadium, Saint John survives through a good stiff dose of pragmatism. For example, facing the staggering sum of $8,000 a month to heat the church for daily mass, they transformed a former schoolroom -- itself a former coal chute -- into a small chapel. Necessity being the mother of the Chapel of the Holy Mother, the little side prayer space, with its own wooden icon screen, does wonderfully well. Facing modernity, it pays homage to the past.

"We're trying to continue this," Father Chirovsky gestures at his lovely little chapel. "We're trying to connect it with our lives."

CHAPTER SIX

IMMACULATE HEART OF MARY CHURCH

An enormous dichotomy rises above the south bank of the Allegheny River. Simply for its sheer physical presence, the Immaculate Heart of Mary Church, its massive copper dome oxidized green, is a commanding landmark up and down the valley -- a reminder of medieval cities, where no building could stand taller, physically or metaphysically, than the church.

Then, in the little village of Polish Hill, the Immaculate Heart of Mary maintains its traditional role as the locus of the community. "What the city does not provide," commented Father John Jendzura, the church's long-time pastor, "the church gives. It gives to people their spiritual needs and the traditions handed over by the forefathers – adapted to the present. We are traditionalists," he added in the late 1970s, just after then-Presidential candidate Jimmy Carter's Brereton Street campaign stop put Polish Hill on the national map, "and we are conservative. But we are outgoing."

Built largely by their own hands, for the people of Polish Hill the Immaculate Heart of Mary is their one fixed point in a changing age. "I never thought about leaving," said lifelong resident Ann Davis. "The church is part of me. I love the church. I didn't want to live anywhere else."

"There's always that loyalty," Father John added. "They brought it from Europe and kept it through the church."

Conceived as a Polish ethnic parish in 1895, as large numbers of Polish immigrants moved up from the Strip to the north edge of Herron Hill, the Immaculate Heart of Mary supplanted the older, more established St. Stanislaus Kostka Church. With the cornerstone of the new combined church, school, and convent laid in October, 1896, the completed building was dedicated a year later.

Originally, the new building's first floor served as the school, the second floor as the church. Yet within two years, the waves of immigrants, and their burgeoning families, had outgrown the church. So in 1899 the parish purchased land from a former brick factory for a larger church. With this second cornerstone laid in 1904, the new, landmark church was finished a year later.

Funded entirely by the working people of the newly named Polish Hill, who gave 25 cents a week out of their grocery money toward construction, the Immaculate Heart of Mary, modeled on St. Peter's Basilica in Rome, cost a princely $160,000. No one doubts

that it would have carried a far heavier price tag had it not been for the endless hours of sweat equity which the community poured into the church: after working all day elsewhere, many men -- carpenters, bricklayers, plasterers -- put in entire second shifts building the church. While their names are unknown today -- as with medieval cathedrals, human agency was deemed unimportant, the work paramount -- they were recorded for posterity and placed in a locket held over Mary's Immaculate Heart above the altar.

Importing their mahogany altar from Chicago, and the stained glass windows from Innsbruck, the images reflect themes of Christ's life – annunciation, birth, death, and resurrection – as well as Mary's assumption into heaven, and numerous Polish saints – Adalbert, Hedwig, Stanislaus Kostka, and others. The Stations of the Cross are in attendance, too, painted on slate, the descriptions in Polish.

The 2,000-seat church opened packed with parishioners -- for Christmas and Easter they had to set up folding chairs to accommodate the crowds. Until 1950, old timers say, they averaged some 1,800 at every service; today, by contrast, a big crowd tops 600 (except for Christmas and Easter, when the flock and their descendents all come home.) Similarly, the school, now closed, once hosted 1,500 students in three buildings.

The bells remain, five huge ones, all rung by hand, all heard easily in the village, of course, and as far off as Bloomfield and Lawrenceville. Rung on Sundays, holidays, and for funerals, like everything in Polish Hill they are the province of experienced, long-termed people, villagers who walk to church, who have worked and retired, and who have seemed to have rung these bells since they arrived from the foundry.

For all its opulence, however, the Immaculate Heart of Mary is configured oddly – the Brereton Avenue doors open in the church's mid-section, not in back, as is usual. Since the baker, who held the adjacent parcel a century ago, wouldn't sell his land to the church, they had to reconfigure the building. And so they built it, and dedicated it -- and watched the bakery burn down. "Maybe it was a sign," shrugs Father Joseph Swierczynski, the current pastor.

A small, modest man dressed in a blue sweat shirt, black shoes, and black trousers, Father Joe, as he's universally known, is a Sharpsburg native who moved to Polish Hill in 1995 after a 19-year posting on the South Side. While he is comfortable celebrating mass in English -- with Polish hymns for some liturgical spice -- his 9:00 AM Sunday mass is entirely Polish, a throwback to the old days. "Every mass," he says proudly, "has some aspect of the Polish language."

And of course of Polish-American culture as well. At the height of World War II, for example, the Immaculate Heart of Mary held special services virtually non-stop (a list of the war dead stands in a memorial shrine outside the building). So important -- and

moving -- were the devotions that both Art Rooney and David Lawrence paid their respects at one time or another.

As did Pope John Paul II, when he was Karol Wojtyla. Coming in 1969 as the Archbishop of Krakow, he was given the honor to unveil a memorial plaque for the Polish scientist and Nobel Laureate Marie Sklodowska Curie.

She's hardly the only great woman honored at the Immaculate Heart of Mary. Holy Family foundress Frances Siedliska is remembered in a death mask -- which is said to be uncannily like her living image. There's Saint Theresa, too, the same French woman who is said to have miraculously cured little Edith Piaf's blindness, and whom Father Joe personally credits for curing him from the ill effects of both a stroke and cancer.

Closer to home, the Immaculate Heart of Mary offers a Devotion to Divine Mercy, the first parish in United States to feature this special novena for Holy Week, Good Friday through the Sunday after Easter. Initiated by Father John Jendzura some 30 years ago, the novena was created by Saint Faustina, a 20th-century nun, visionary, and mystic who was born Helena Kowalska and was initiated as Sister Maria Faustina. Receiving visions of Christ and Mary, she wrote that Jesus revealed to her His purpose: to spread the devotion of the Mercy of God. Beatified in 1993, and canonized in 2000, Saint Faustina's Divine Mercy Sunday, celebrated the first Sunday after Easter, centers around a novena which Christ himself dictated to her. Written in her diary, it was initially banned by the Church, but later canonized. So powerful are her words that Cardinal Franciszek Macharski, John Paul II's successor as Archbishop of Krakow, said that the work "reminds us of the gospel we had forgotten."

The faithful come from as far as Johnstown for these special Devotions, and for all of the Blessed Mother's Feast Days – the annunciation, assumption, and so on. "On Christmas," Father Joe says, "people come from everywhere," in part because the church is graced with 100 trees. For Easter, he still blesses the baskets on Holy Saturday -- just as they've done for a century and more. "It's packed on that day, too," he says.

"The beauty of this Church draws people here," Father Joe adds. "As does the liturgy – it's not something that we just slap together. We create it carefully -- and we draw people from all over. It's Polish," he nods. "It's the church itself."

CHAPTER SEVEN

MUSLIM COMMUNITY CENTER OF GREATER PITTSBURGH

A-salaam aleikum, the natty little man says to a group of T-shirted boys, here this summer morning at the Muslim Community Center for camp and *Al-Qur'an*.
Aleikum salaam, they answer smartly.
In a large, glass-walled room in suburban Monroeville, the boys gather 'round for their daily lesson before a bit of fun in the sun.
On a woodsy, suburban site, in a decidedly modern-looking building whose crescent moons atop entrance announce its Islamic purpose, the boys study beneath flags of the 20 countries from which their parents hail -- Egypt, Syria, Jordan, Iraq, Malaysia, Uzbekistan, Turkey, Lebanon, and more. Committed to Abrahamic teachings, they learn that Islam, like many other religions, has at its heart the surrender of one's will to God's -- and therefore finding peace.
They understand this from many sources, from all the prophets of the Bible and *Al-Qur'an*. Following the Islamic belief that God sent Moses, David, Jesus, and Mohammed to educate humanity, the boys listen intently. "You have to believe in the four books," explains Dr. Pir M. Toor, the diminutive, gentle, soft-spoken president of the Muslim Community Center of Greater Pittsburgh. An English-educated Pakistani, he adds that such belief -- along with monotheism, prayer, charity, and Haj (the once-in-a-lifetime pilgrimage to Mecca) -- is one the articles of faith, one of the Five Pillars of Islam.
First, he explains, there is the *shahadah*, or creed, which, translated from Arabic into English, proclaims that "I testify that there is none worthy of worship except God, and I testify that Mohammed is the Messenger of God."
To focus on God, he continues, one must engage in *salah*, prayer, five times a day, each time facing Mecca. Understood as a personal communication with God, all the prayers -- Arabic verses from *Al Qur'an* -- encompass both gratitude and worship. *Zakat*, or charity, another pillar, is particularly important to Dr. Toor and the Community Center, for these mandatory donations both help the poor as well as spread a general understanding of Islam.
Yet even a few decades ago, such understanding had little import -- there was virtually no Sunni Muslim culture in Pittsburgh, very little even in the United States. Having emigrated to the United States to work as a nuclear engineer, it was a lonely place for Dr. Toor, his family, and his co-religionists. Finally, in 1987, with a critical mass of

families in place, they needed a suitable place for worship and education. Buying a small house on a suburban two-acre plot, within four years, 1991, they added the social hall where his young charges are meeting this morning. Six years after that, 1997, the Community Center added a second building dedicated for worship and education. It was Pittsburgh's first indigenous Islamic center.

"It was supported by the community," Dr. Toor says. "No money came from anybody else." He shrugs. "We didn't need it."

The group, he adds, was much like Dr. Toor himself -- almost exclusively professionals. Engineers, physicians, university professors; MDs and PhDs -- "we were all first immigrants," Dr. Toor recalls. "At that time, the majority of our 50 families were from Pakistan, India, Afganistan, and Bangladesh. While we built this as a worship center for the Muslim community, we conducted things according to our traditions."

Initially desiring to limit membership in order to preserve the Muslim culture specific to their four countries of origin, the Community Center was challenged by Muslims from other countries who wanted to join. Although there was push-back from some of the founders, still, Dr. Toor says, "you cannot deny any Muslim who wants to come to a mosque. People who live in this area are welcome to worship."

Welcoming all Muslims, the Community Center quickly grew four-fold. Now 200 families strong, and growing, the group is independent of any national origin or particular tradition. "We have a good organization," Dr. Toor says. "We get along very well."

They get along in a decidedly Spartan place – there is none of the riot of color so prevalent in other houses of worship; there are no seats, statues, or stained glass. There are no distractions. Instead, in this modest, carpeted hall, there are strategically placed bookcases and sayings on the walls, the members pray five times daily, kneeling shoeless, facing east, toward Mecca.

Washing their faces, heads, arms, and feet before prayer, they segregate by gender, the women upstairs in their own balcony.

Inclusiveness, Dr. Toor gestures, has been the key to their growth, to their Muslim faith itself. As such, in addition to its own internal education programming, the Community Center has undertaken external education as well, engaging in a series of interfaith dialogues with non-Muslims about America's fastest-growing religion.

"The basic thing in the world is ignorance of each other's faith," Dr. Toor says sadly. To counter that, the Community Center has engaged in outreach endeavors with Jewish, Hindu, Christian, and Zoroastrian congregations, teaching about Islam, stressing tolerance, searching for common ground. "We have very good relations with other religious groups," Dr. Toor says proudly.

That even includes the FBI. One Sunday in April, 2009, some 200 people and an FBI team met at the Community Center for a picnic. Before a group largely made up of people of South Asian, Arab, and East African descent, Nawar Shora, an FBI Consultant, and Special Agent Jim Knights had an hour-long discussion ranging over a wide variety of topics, from career opportunities to community concerns.

Receiving high marks for such outreach activities, notably those with the Jewish community, Dr. Toor is heartened by his mosque's role in spreading a greater understanding of Islam -- especially in post-911, post-Fort Hood times, when there is so much distrust, so much misunderstanding about Islam itself, and about the differences between the more normative, more tolerant Sunni branch of Islam, and other, more xenophobic forms.

"People are trying to understand each other," he says. "Their minds are open and inquisitive. They are very interested. Knowing your own roots -- while understanding others -- is very important."

CHAPTER EIGHT

ST. LOUISE DE MARILLAC CHURCH

It's one of life's delicious ironies that a chapel that began as an idea, as an expression of a woman's private devotion, has become one of Pittsburgh's more popular Catholic churches -- and one of the region's most intimate, and inspiring, houses of worship.

In the Nineteenth Century, certainly by 1880, part of what is now Upper St. Clair was the Baldesberger farm. By the mid-Twentieth Century, when such large tracts were being sold for housing, Walter and Mary Baldesberger still maintained the family holdings. Devout Catholics, they were regulars at church, no one more than Mary, who had a special attachment to St. Francis of Assisi, especially his work with the poor, people broken by economic and emotional hardship.

As time trimmed the property, Mary Baldesberger -- and the Pittsburgh diocese -- never lost sight of her dream, that someday there would be a church on Baldesberger land.

After her husband died in 1954, and as the farm was being dissolved, Mary Baldesberger got her wish -- when, in 1961, Bishop John Wright established a church on land purchased from the estate. Not naming it for Saint Francis -- there were already Sisters of Saint Francis in the area -- instead, he named the new parish for a relatively new saint, a woman, Saint Louise de Marillac.

Wise and sensitive, the bishop felt that she was a fitting role model for women, as well as a noble way to honor Mary Baldesberger. Born out of wedlock in 1591, Louise de Marillac grew up wealthy and well educated. Married, the mother of a son, after her husband's death, and under the direction of her mentor Vincent de Paul, she began working with women to aid the poor, eventually founding the Daughters of Charity, officially approbated in 1655.

So good were they at pastoral care, that the Daughters achieved unprecedented success at the Hotel-Dieu, then Paris' oldest and largest hospital. Under her tutelage, the Daughters expanded their scope of services to include work in orphanages, prisons, old-age and mental asylums, and, presaging both Florence Nightingale and Clara Barton by some 200 years, on battlefields.

After increasingly ill health, 68-year-old Louise de Marillac died in 1660, six months before the death of Vincent de Paul. By that time, however, her Daughters of Charity

ran more than 40 French institutions. Today, the Daughters of Charity, Sisters of Charity, Ladies of Charity, and many offshoots literally cover the globe.

Beatified by Pope Benedict XV in 1920, in 1934 Louise de Marillac was canonized by Pope Pius XI. As a further honor, she was declared Patroness of Christian Social Workers by Pope John XXIII in 1960.

The following year, Bishop Wright, only two years into his Pittsburgh position, established her parish, first in the large white Baldesberger farmhouse, which became a convent for the Felician Sisters, a Franciscan order, later in a renovated farm equipment building. Constructing a proper building to serve as a church and school, on Christmas Day, 1963, the first mass was celebrated in the newly established Saint Louise de Marillac Church -- 303 years after her passing.

As Upper St. Clair grew -- some of it from the Baldesberger farm being converted into houses -- Reverend Robert Reardon, who became pastor in 1978, articulated the need for a larger church. Retaining local architect Lucian Caste, they set about designing a new building.

With the cornerstone laid in 1980, the new Saint Louise de Marillac Church opened on August 23, 1981.

What Caste created was entirely different from the previous church -- and something unique in the region. In the deceptively small-looking chapel, which actually seats a robust 750, worshippers found basic materials -- wood, glass, steel, and stone -- awash in primary colors from stained glass more inspirational than representational. Beautiful without being overwhelming, "it *is* stunning," says church sacristan Mary Weaver.

Although the rough-cut altar stones are actually from Somerset, they give the church a Holy Land feel, as if they were quarried there. For some, the altar is reminiscent of Jerusalem; for others, Weaver says, "it reminds them of catacombs."

With the Hunt Studios' stained glass windows in deep reds and yellows, including an imaginative rendering of Saint Louise, the light is muted, diffused. "At different times of the day," Weaver says, "the wood has a different tone to it."

At the time the church was dedicated, Lucian Caste and Jim Heim wrote of the church's extraordinary interplay of light and dark: "light enters and fades, darkness sets in, then suddenly the space, the structure, the nave and the Christocentric axis are apparent once more. The way returns to the beginning. At the beginning and the end stands the portal."

With the cumulative effect a cool, somber room, reflective as opposed to narrative, Saint Louise de Marillac draws its strength from being suggestive, from being quiet and contemplative. Worshippers are induced, rather than impelled, to prayer.

"The Liturgical Space," Caste and Heim added, "the total inner space of the church, is meant to communicate a sense of integrity. It is the space of Sacred Abundance which

warms people and gives them a sense of tenderness towards one another. There is a sense of personal scale and spiritual uplift; warm and hospitable that encourages community worship."

According to the energetic, engaged pastor, Father Michael Caridi, that community is strong -- and growing stronger every day.

Currently, St. Louise de Marillac regularly celebrates private masses, two to three weddings every weekend during spring and summer, and three baptisms virtually every Sunday. Recently, the church welcomed some 150 children for first communion; 168 for confirmation. Some 400 children are enrolled in the adjacent school.

Regularly drawing 3,000 people to six weekend masses, the congregation represents the depth and breadth of Pittsburgh. "They're all different," Weaver says. "The area is really growing -- there are a lot of generational families here. And the masses are packed. It's incredible."

Yet Saint Louise de Marillac is also a private place, drawing people who may be in the public eye, but who, during services, prefer to shun the spotlight. "While I can't list specific names of people who worship here," Father Caridi understandably says, "there are many accomplished people who pass through our doors regularly. It is not uncommon to see local star athletes, politicians, and TV personalities attending mass or funeral services at Saint Louise. Also, many leaders of local industries call Saint Louise their home parish" -- and they, too, prefer their devotions to be discreet.

"Our church opens every morning at 6 A.M.," he smiles, "and doesn't close until 11:30 P.M. You can always find someone in the church praying or meditating." Father Caridi pauses to glance about at the rich woods, the strong steel beams, the stones, the omnipresent and ever-changing light. "Our church is very conducive to private prayer," much akin to Mary Baldesberger's dream, which came to full fruition decades later.

CHAPTER NINE

First Hungarian Reformed Church of Homestead

He apologizes that his English isn't very good, although it's fine; English, he says, is his second language. Hungarian is his first. (He was born and educated there, and came to this country only after the 1956 revolution failed.)

He apologizes that his is a vanishing congregation, ethnic churches being a thing of the past. The young people are worshipping elsewhere -- if they're worshipping anywhere at all, he says -- and besides, they don't speak Hungarian. What's more, this isn't the Old Country. Whatever Hungary once was, what's here are distant, dying memories.

He apologizes that the young people no longer stay married. A fleeting smile, a stray bit of sunlight peeking through century-old stained glass: he adds that he's been married for a solid half-century. And counting.

He apologizes that he's more or less retired, more rather than less these days, and comes to the old church in Homestead but once a week, on Sundays, and only for religious services. Otherwise, he's home, in Brownsville, which, given his age and its distance, might as well be on the other side of the world. When he's not at the church in the old neighborhood, the building stands locked, its steel-sheathed spire a wraith above the river.

He apologizes that the church's name, the Hungarian Reformed Church of Homestead, is somewhat misleading. It's not really in Homestead, not anymore. "Not since they moved the boundary line," Reverend Alexander Jalso says. "It's in Munhall now."

Churches like Homestead's Hungarian Reformed come from a time when third place really was church, when people put their hearts and souls, every spare nickel, and every available hour into them. Built on workers' wages and pennies cribbed from milk money, these were created by lunch-bucket laymen, for whom vacations meant piling everyone into the hot-as-an-open-hearth family flivver and high-flying to Cousin Herky's in Altoona for Fourth of July.

For these people, many of whom arrived from Europe with their hearts full of hope and their belongings tied in rags, the church's annual Lawn Fête, held on dusty sideyards or asphalt parking lots, was hard-scrapple Ascot, a ne'er-to-be-missed event where the skilled, and the blessed, could win a fresh vegetable basket that kept their families in red cabbage and white potatoes for a week.

A century-and-a-half ago, the First Hungarian Reformed Church began as a small group of Hungarians living in and around Downtown and the Hill. Bringing the Calvinist tradition from Europe, by 1889 they had formed the First Magyar and Slovak Evangelical Lutheran and Reformed St. Paul Church. Within a year, the two ethnic groups split, half forming the Pittsburgh and Vicinity First Hungarian Reformed Church. In 1891 they hired the Reverend John Kovacs for the princely sum of $600 per annum. Within another year, 1892, they had dropped the Vicinity from the name and the newly minted Hungarian Reformed Church of Pittsburgh moved into a wooden building on Oakland's Bates Street. After moving across Oakland, then to Hazelwood, in 1903 a splinter group crossed the Monongahela, there to found the First Hungarian Reformed Church of Homestead.

On May 24, 1903, Reverend Sandor Harsanyi -- a kindly, bearded man with thinning hair and deep-set eyes -- convened a meeting in the small, wooden Fourth Street Lutheran Church. He had found a property, on Tenth Avenue, on the hillside overlooking the two-mile-long steel mill and the river, nestled in a residential area that would shortly host no less than 15 other churches. It was a good location, two long blocks away from the bumps and bustle, the honky-tonks and hardware stores of Eighth Avenue. The church elders -- a group of men cut in a pattern of black hair, black mustaches, black ties, black suits, wearing stern and steely expressions on their square-cut faces -- agreed, and, purchasing the land for $14,250, began construction on April 18, 1904, laying the cornerstone two months later.

Building a smaller, more intimate church than their model, the Hungarian Reformed Church on Budapest's Calvin Square, they replicated the single steeple, the trademark pillars and pediment, this one with an angel watching beneficently as the faithful ascend the steep concrete steps to enter the warm, intimate chapel. Inside, they added Gothic windows, Romanesque arches, and Hungarian grace notes, including a stained glass window of a typical Hungarian village church.

With construction costs said to be $30,000, they dedicated the church the following Reformation Sunday, October 30, the ceremony entirely in Hungarian. "This day," Reverend Harsanyi said, "will be a memory in our hearts, the Church a light forever for the Magyars who have settled in this country. We ask you who have settled here in a far-away unknown land to preserve your fathers' scared inheritance; do not allow

indifference and uninvolvement to break, as would an enemy, the branches from the tree of the Church."

By 1907, the congregation was flourishing: that year alone, they celebrated 107 weddings -- and, not surprisingly, 197 baptisms the next.

By 1950, the church needed some touch-up, including adding the distinctive stainless steel sheath atop its spire, topped with a star, recalling the Star of Bethlehem, calling the faithful to prayer.

In 1952, the year the church began having separate English and Hungarian services, the artist Joseph Kolozi was paid $1,000 to decorate the interior of the sanctuary, including the half-dome over the altar. Using geometric and floral motifs, he included many Christian symbols, the lamb, dove, harp, crown, rock, star, chalice, and so on, all small, subtle reminders of the faith. "It's quite unique," comments George Kohl, the church's veteran organist.

Until the Second World War, Reverend Jalso says, " Hungarian dominated." Then they switched over to English, everything except the traditional Hungarian prayers and hymns.

Now, just two families in the church were born in Hungary; the rest are descendents, some third and fourth generation. "It's getting smaller," he shakes his head. "We are losing members and can't do anything about it."

It is early Sunday morning, nearly time for services. After putting on his black tie, Reverend Jalso has to prepare for his ministry. First step, stuffing his black suit jacket with Hershey nuggets, mini Snickers, and the like. Later, when he gives them to the children, he'll cut each a deal. "I'll be a good boy," he'll wink. "You be a good boy, too. If you are, see me after services. I'll give you another."

"I can't help it," he shrugs. "I love the little ones."

The streets are quiet; the churches nearby deserted. Virtually no cars pass on Tenth Avenue. Out of the morning rain, two frail, elderly people help each other up the steep concrete steps, passing the sign that reads *Isten Hozott* -- you are welcome.

"We wish to keep the legacy of our fathers," Reverend Jalso wrote not so long ago, "preserve the heritage of the previous generations, and keep the faith we learned from our mother and in the church. We are grateful to God for our past and ask His blessing upon our future."

CHAPTER TEN

TEMPLE EMANUEL OF SOUTH HILLS

The very first words that God speaks at the beginning of the Torah are 'Let there be light,'" architect Dan Rothschild says, then gestures at his new sanctuary, a revolutionary round prayer space at Temple Emanuel of South Hills, where the morning sun sends rainbows across the ceiling (themselves symbols of God's covenant with mankind after the Flood), while the setting sun lights the opposite wall on fire. On the floor, a crescent pattern mirrors the moon – a classic Jewish symbol of time passing, of mutability, of renewal.

A contemporary master, Rothschild is quietly reshaping the landscape of Jewish Pittsburgh. From Oakland's Jewish University Center (where the Biblical pillar of fire and hovering cloud greet students on Forbes Avenue), to Squirrel Hill's Shaare Torah Congregation (where his reconfiguration of the half-century-old sanctuary added depth and dignity to a traditional sacred space), to Temple Emanuel of South Hills, and many more, his imaginative union of art and architecture draws not only on strictly Jewish sources, but, perhaps more strikingly, does *not* draw upon Christian sources of art, architecture, and inspiration -- as virtually every American Jewish house of worship has for more than two centuries.

In his newer, more indigenous paradigm, Rothschild uses glass, but not representational stained glass, to which some object as Biblically forbidden graven images. Instead, as part of one wall he designed seven windows representing the days of Creation, each with its own symbol for light, growing things, man, the Sabbath, and so on. Over the ark that contains the traditional Torah scrolls, as he did in Oakland Rothschild fashioned a bronze cover to recall the pillar of fire, and a curtain for the cloud, that led the Jewish people through the desert in *Exodus*. With the room surrounded outdoors by 12 pillars, ranging from four to 40 feet high, representing the Jewish people's 12 Tribes, the curves of the walls themselves suggest the Torah scrolls.

"He's in the tradition of the Biblical architects Betzalel and Oholiav, who constructed the *mishkan*, the traveling tabernacle," Temple Emanuel's Rabbi Mark Mahler says. "He's making God's tent."

This version of God's tent, so to speak, moved to the South Hills in May, 1951, when a small group of Jewish families began their own Reform congregation. In the ensuing six decades, as Temple Emanuel grew to 600 families, the building, like Topsy, grew, too, in four iterations.

After meeting in spacious homes, neighboring schools, and hospitable churches, the congregation settled on Bower Hill Road. From the 1954 cornerstone laying, through the 1960 expansion, another addition in 1991, finally to the Rothschild millennium, "the synagogue," Rabbi Mahler says, "exists for what goes on in it."

Combining prayer, Torah study, and social action, Temple Emanuel is noted for its spectrum of activities -- from Rabbi Mahler's justly famous guitar-led services to the congregation's leadership in such relief causes as Hurricanes Andrew and Katrina, Darfur, and many others. "Judaism," Rabbi Mahler gestures, "is a religion that pushes you into the world."

And into its art, if Temple Emanuel is any yardstick. From the outset, Temple Emanuel wed itself to the rich ecclesiastical tradition of stained glass. In 1961, for example, the congregation imported 26 brilliantly colored and highly symbolic windows from the noted Parisian artist Robert Pinart. For *Rosh Hashana* (the New Year), for example, Pinart blended dark red with orange, blue, and green, culminating in white to symbolize faith and hope. By comparison, his panel for *Yom Kippur* (the Day of Atonement) depicts fasting and soul searching in somber, meditative purple, blue, and gray.

For *Pesach* (Passover), his imaginative rendering of the quintessential festival of freedom, combining spring's earthly renewal with God's deliverance of the Jewish people from Egyptian slavery, spins in warm, seasonal colors. For *Shavuos*, (Pentecost, or the Festival of Weeks), Pinart's vertical blue and white lines suggest Mt. Sinai, the traditional place that God gave the Jewish people the Torah. Atop, 10 ten horizontal clear and white panes symbolize the Ten Commandments, which God carved and Moses brought down to the Jewish people.

To such inspirational glasswork, noted Pittsburgh artist Jerry Caplan added three sets of wood and ceramic panels. For the latter, "The Seeds of Promise," he sculpted a seed pod in various stages of opening. Symbolizing past, present, and future, the seed pod suggests the fullness of life and its infinite potential.

Using traditional symbols appropriate to each usage, for "Heritage of Holidays," Caplan's set of six carved wood panels -- birch finished in walnut -- represents the major Jewish holidays. His "Twelve Tribes of Israel" uses 12 birch panels, carved on both sides for vision from any angle, finished to look like butternut. Taken as a set, the two represent the rich Jewish holiday tradition -- and the bounteous blessings given to the Jewish people.

Along the same lines, Thomas Brunger used brass, slate, and stainless steel in his nine-foot "L'Chaim" (to life) to symbolize unity, light and inspiration -- all in the deep roots of Jewish heritage. At the sculpture's core, a hexagon comprises 18 major triangles and 384 small triangles -- transformed into the traditional Star of David.

Also working in metal, James Frape decorated the older, more traditional, rectilinear main sanctuary, designed in 1960, with representations of the Ten Commandments, *Menorah* (candelabra), *Ner Tamid* (eternal light), Torah crowns, Wine Goblet, and Star of David. Using hammered brass, the *Menorah*, for example, is tree-like in shape, its central shaft and arms appearing like almond flowers, Aaron's symbol as figured in his staff. Similarly, Frape's *Ner Tamid* appears as a pomegranate, its dozen amber seeds symbolizing Israel's Twelve Tribes.

Into this rich tradition of evocative but non-representation art, Rothschild added his own architectural finesse, including forming his *Beit HaT'filah* (house of prayer, or sanctuary) of opposing curvilinear walls. While the eastern wall, a simple arc radiating from a central point, represents the singularity of God, the western wall, a compound curve consisting of several arcs, represents the diversity of the community. For true prayer, Judaism says, we need both.

Outside the *Beit HaT'filah*, the site walls slope downward and curl inward, like two arms, hearkening back to God's outstretched arm which took the Jewish people out of Egypt.

Still outdoors, the brick site walls in the courtyard begin narrow but grow increasingly taller and wider, until they become a broad sweeping plane pointing to the sky -- representing the spiritual progress of man. For the specifically Jewish element, Rothschild embedded 613 colored pebbles in the bricks, each piece of glass representing one of the Torah's 613 *mitzvot* (commandments).

As Rothschild envisions it, as members of Temple Emanuel walk through the courtyard, the fountain *here* symbolizing man's covenant with man, the 12 Tribes' concrete pillars *there* symbolizing man's covenant with God, they will be sufficiently inspired to prepare themselves for prayer.

CHAPTER ELEVEN

PITTSBURGH NEW CHURCH

The pre-history of the Pittsburgh New Church, in Point Breeze, goes back to Pittsburgh myth and manufacturing. First the myth, dating back to the early days of the Republic when a young fellow named John Chapman decided to go into the seed business. As an increasingly larger number of settlers populated the greater Ohio Valley, and points west, Chapman traveled hither and yon selling apple seeds. An average sort of fellow who blanketed the western part of Pennsylvania, by 1790 he had been introduced to the Swedenborgian strain of Christianity in Greensburg. Turning to Faithe and Workes as a path to salvation, and adopting Emmanuel Swedenborg's idea of being useful, Chapman began hauling about Swedenborgian tracts, handing them out wily-wily, even tearing pages out of books and giving them away if he felt the words would have an impact. Simultaneously, as he began giving away seeds to his tart green rambos, which subsequently sprang up all about the region, Chapman earned the sobriquet Johnny Appleseed.

What Chapman was selling came from the writings of Emanuel Swedenborg, a Swedish scientist, engineer, and spiritualist. Born in 1688, Swedenborg was a mining engineer who also helped build locks and dams for river navigation. Retiring in 1745, he devoted himself to Bible study, both Hebrew and Christian. Beginning to have profound spiritual experiences, including self-described prophecy and visions of Heaven, Swdenborg carefully recorded them; *in toto* they amount to a reworking of what he called the old Christian Church. As his foundation for a new Christianity -- and his General Church of the New Jerusalem -- Swedenborg produced some 18 books, with

more published posthumously.

James Glen, a British Swedenborgian, brought his books to Philadelphia in 1784. There, and elsewhere, book clubs gradually developed into more organized churches, as it happened in the western part of the state, through Greensburg, Johnny Appleseed, and travelers everywhere.

The ideas, as well as the apple seeds, took root, Swedenborg's visions of Heaven and the New Jerusalem sweeping the Midwest, notably in Ohio and Michigan. "There was a lot of interest in spiritism," comments the Pittsburgh New Church's Pastor Amos Glenn. "Swedenborg talked to spirits and visited Heaven. That was much more accepted at face value than it is today."

As Pittsburgh morphed from a sleepy frontier trading post into an industrial juggernaut, Swedenborgian readers dotted the area, so many of them that by 1848 they attracted a young Scots immigrant named William Carnegie, who brought his wee laddie, 13-year-old Andrew, who studied Swendenborgian theology -- and even sang in the choir.

Although the idea didn't take in young master Carnegie, it did in some of his more powerful contemporaries, including the Phipps, McCandless, and Childs families. (For example, Carnegie's one-time partner's wife, Mrs. Henry Clay Frick -- Adelaide Howard Childs -- was a Swedenborgian.) Similarly, John Pitcairn, co-founder of Pittsburgh Plate Glass, was a lifelong New Church member and generous supporter, as was architect Daniel Burnham, whose Pittsburgh landmarks include the Pennsylvania Railroad Station, the Frick Building, and the Oliver Building.

By 1885 the congregation had built a handsome church in Allegheny, near where the Andy Warhol Museum stands today. Then, of course, there was the inevitable schism. (While it's true that, following the famous dictum, all church steeples point in the same direction, it's equally true that sooner or later those who sit in the pews will go their various ways.) By 1900, one faction had moved to an Amberson Street home, in Shadyside, and 29 years later laid a foundation stone on Le Roi Road, Point Breeze. Within a decade they had their own signature building, the Pitcairn family providing the lion's share of the leadership and largesse.

While there are ornate New Church buildings elsewhere, "this style is more typical," Pastor Glenn says of his church that resembles nothing so much as an English country chapel: the stripped-down Tudor features plain walls, wood beams and wainscoting, and stone arches. "The focus of our worship is not ornamental," he adds, "so it's not about creating the most elaborate space you can. Instead, the focus is instruction, prayer, and praise. So the idea is to create a space that is conducive to that worship."

"We're lucky to have a space that's beautiful," Pastor Glenn smiles. "What makes it a sacred space is the use that it serves."

Pointing to the small, Spartan altar, Pastor Glenn notes that it has three steps, with each step having three layers -- like the Trinity, certainly, but also like a human being. "We have three parts," he says, "soul, body, and the things that we do. Similarly, a life is made of things you love, things you know, things you do. Here, you'll see a lot of those threes around."

Small stained glass windows above the altar are the New Church story writ small -- one panel shows the New Church that Swedenborg saw in Heaven. The panel with the communion wafer recalls the Passover unleavened bread, with the Hebrew letter *hey* represents the human acceptance of God's spirit -- as Abram becomes Abraham and Sarai becomes Sarah in *Genesis* -- along with the biblical concept that God's breath animates human beings.

On the altar itself stands a large book, *The Word*, containing both the Hebrew and Christian Bibles. A seven-branched candelabra represents *Revelation* -- as well as Swedenborg's own description of the coming of the New Church and of the New Jerusalem.

In the back, an offertory for donations, like those freely given by the Hebrews to build the Tabernacle, similarly serves a holy purpose. "It's a completely free will offering," Pastor Glenn says, "given to the Lord for His purpose, for His use."

Some of the use is the New Church's own K-8 school, which first opened in 1885, and has predictably risen and fallen with the times. (By necessity, it was all-volunteer during the Depression, when enrollment dropped to a mere 10.) "The message has a lot to do with self-identity," he says. "We're bringing up two dozen children to be people who become angels."

With current membership hovering somewhere shy of the six-dozen mark, Pastor Glenn admits that the going can get tough in a decidedly secular age. "Outreach is a struggle," he sighs. "You've got to start with the belief that what Emmanuel Swedenborg wrote are the words of God equal in authenticity to the Old Testament and the New Testament. That he was a prophet. Lots of people have trouble with that." He pauses. "Understandably so."

Thoughts of Heaven aside, it's time to ring the bell, which Pastor Glenn does himself, at 11 every Sunday morning, calling the faithful to worship. "We might be the only New Church with a bell," he shrugs.

As the congregants enter, they come through a door framed by a pomegranate and a bell, biblical symbols of plentitude and prayer. "We all have that Children of Israel stuff in us," Pastor Glenn says. "We all have battles to fight.

"The story of the journey to the land of Canaan is the story of our journey to Heaven."

CHAPTER TWELVE

Sri Venkateswara Temple

They imported architects and artisans from their native India to get it right, this sparkling white building on a hilltop overlooking the Parkway East, the carvings, statuary, all visible from the roadway below.
A closer look reveals stairs marked in colors, patterns, a riot of design, of symbol. It is a weekday mid-afternoon, but people come and go, visitors, regulars, some in western clothes, others in traditional Indian garb, billowing shirts, saris, and robes, multicolored fabrics, a flowing river of bright colors, shades, and hues.
Although both this temple and its brother in New York claim to be the first authentic Hindu structure in North America, both arriving in late 1976, it is safe to say that Sri Venkateswara Temple is Pittsburgh's first. Modeled on a famous temple in Tirupati, Andhra Pradesh, India, it is a startling replica of classic, seventh-century Indian art and architecture, a worship space dedicated to its deity, Vishnu. (A major Hindu deity, Vishnu, Sanskrit for Omnipresent, has 10 forms, or avatars, nine of which are believed to have come to the universe. The 10th, a messianic being, will arrive "to straighten the mess we have made," explains Ramaswamy Raghavan, native of Chennai, India, docent, devotée, and retired Dravo chemical engineer. Much like other religions, he adds, Hinduism posits a divine being who will come to Earth and lead people to Providence.) Caretaker of the universe, Vishnu more or less shares duties with Brahma, the creator, and Shiva, the destroyer. As expressed in the four Vedas, or scriptures, the deities are also figured in time -- Brahma (past), Vishnu (present), Shiva (future).
For something so ornate, the million-dollar temple had a surprisingly short gestation period. It was barely 40 years ago that a Hindu Temple Society formed in New York to assure proper worship in proper structures in the New World. By 1972, there was sufficient local demand for true Hindu culture that the House of India, on Squirrel Hill's Forward Avenue, offered both traditional dance classes as well as a *de facto* worship space, including a Lord Ganesa deity.
As the Pittsburgh Hindu community grew -- fueled largely by high-level employees at Dravo, Westinghouse, and other engineering-construction corporations -- by 1973 they had formed their own Hindu Temple Society, founding dues $300, and had begun creating plans for a formal temple. With the June 30, 1976, groundbreaking conducted according to strict Hindu rites, the Indian architects and artisans traveled to fashion it, 15 in the first wave, 15 in the second. Why not simply hire local talent -- or build it from scratch? Impossible, Raghavan says: temples must be built

according to strict *Agama Sastras* (temple manuals.) "There are *rules* to Hindu architecture," he gestures.

Some four-and-a-half months later, November 17, 1976, the temple opened. Essentially shaped like divine being lying horizontally -- red doors entry, stairs rising, a pillar with Vishnu's red mark, concentric sacred spaces -- "the idea is that there a chance for us to become one with divine beings," Raghavan says.

Here, the resident deity, Venkateswara (Lord of Venkata, a representation of Vishnu) rests in the innermost recess called the Garbhagraha (most holy space). However, before we get there, let's walk through what they call S.V. Temple by the numbers:

First, one enters through a Door, much like feet stretched out, walking shoeless, beginning the worship experience.

Second, one ascends to a Platform, readying oneself for an encounter with the divine.

Third, one encounters a Pillar, a stone topped with a copper square, the forehead of red, Vishnu's mark, his shield and conch on the sides. On the back, an eagle, his transport.

Fourth, one enters the Great Hall, a large space reserved for prayer.

Fifth, one enters a smaller room, the Ante Chamber, with statuary guards outside the door. Here, one encounters Mother Earth (Sri Andal, or Sri Bhoodevi, Goddess of the Earth), two wives flanking the antechamber, holding forth the blessings of beauty, spiritual and material wealth. Here we also see Sri Padmavathi, the Goddess of Wealth, with lotus flowers for hands.

Sixth, and last, one peers into the Deity Chamber, for only ordained priests may enter. There, in this temple dedicated to Vishnu, is his statue, on his traditional lotus, holding his symbolic shield and conch. Guarding, supporting, him, his wife Lakshmi is carved over the door -- as are what Raghavan terms "manifestations of him in various forms" on the doors, five on each side. As always, Vishnu has his shield on his right shoulder, ready for defense; on his left, his conch, Vishnu's clarion call for knowledge, for wisdom. Finally, Vishnu's right hand points to the ground -- come to me, he says.

This is all according to the Agama, which states that Narayana, the eternal Divine Being, should be worshipped in the Archa Roopam (iconic form) in temples and homes. Like the temple itself, the deities all originate in the Old Country, being carved and consecrated in India, then shipped overseas in boxes packed with rice. Even though once they are given life by a priest, the deities cannot lose their power, nevertheless they can flag a bit due to transgressions committed by priests or participants, and so may need to be re-energized.

But that is for another time. Today, like every day, a tilak, or mark, of white ash on his forehead means that Raghavan has prayed to Shiva; a dab of red indicates his ablutions toward Vishnu. The symbolism: the divine being resides within him.

In nearly three dozen years, attendance at the S.V. Temple has grown from a relative handful to a few thousand people. Further, given its renowned architecture, and deities, S.V. Temple has become a major stop on the North American Hindu circuit, drawing visitors from all over the continent. "A lot of people come," Raghavan says.

They come in part for daily worship, which has been performed continuously since the building's 1976 dedication. Open in daylight -- meaning nearly 12 hours in the summer -- there is always an India-born Hindu priest on the premises for services. This, too, is according to Agama, which requires a priest not only conduct morning, afternoon, and evening services, but also act as an intermediary between the worshipper and the divine. In down times, the four priests residing at S.V. Temple sit barefoot on a Great Hall carpet, studying holy texts.

For all that level of detail and devotion, though, Raghavan says that one doesn't really need it. "If the divine being lives within you," he says, "you don't need another temple." However, S.V. Temple exists "to expand thinking and worship," he says. "You need a place to ask for blessing. You need a place to meet people."

At the end of the day, Raghavan says, even with all the prayers, the service, the theology; the splendid art and architecture, it all comes down to Karma. "Whatever you do," he says, "you get. It's the tree that grows and gives you shade. You do your duty. Good takes care of itself."

CHAPTER THIRTEEN
ZEN CENTER OF PITTSBURGH

As karmic things go, if you wanted a place for a Zen Center – somewhere that engenders deep meditation and the simple life – then Deep Spring Temple could not be more fitting. Perched on a multi-acre hilltop overlooking Big Sewickley Creek Valley, amidst Western Pennsylvania's rolling verdant hills, Deep Spring Temple is quiet, rustic, contemplative, a bit of peace far from Pittsburgh's madding crowds.

Founded in 1999, the Zen Center is the creation of Kyoki -- née Christine -- Roberts, scioness of the Roberts Jewelry family, who was raised in these parts, wandered the world, then returned home, there to buy her aunt's suburban cottage and transform it into a Zen temple.

A large woman sporting robes, shaved head, and an easy, gentle laugh, the Reverend Roberts -- or, as she insists, Kyoki -- has had many stops along the Zen highway. Traveling west to study agriculture, she married, bore a son, operated a 150-acre Nebraska-based organic hog farm with her then-husband. Divorced, the Episcopalean-raised Kyoki embarked upon a spiritual quest that took her to Minnesota, California (where else?), and Japan. "I was never in modern Japan," she smiles. "I was in 13th-century Japan."

Undergoing a highly rigorous course of study, Kyoki's labors included carrying a bowl and a bell and begging for food. "We called on She Who Hears the Cries of the World," Kyoki recalls, "asking for compassion for the people in the house. We would say that three times and then go on to the next house. Sometimes the people would come out and put money in the bowl or bring rice or vegetables or fruit."

Ordained in the early '90s, after a 30-year absence she returned to Pittsburgh to establish her ministry. "When I first came," Kyoki recalls, " I rented a place by a lake.

Hung out my shingle. Got up every morning, said *zazen* (a 75-minute, lotus-position meditation), and people showed up."

Having a one-year lease, Kyoki began casting about for a more permanent home -- if anything can be called permanent in Zen Buddhism. "This," she gestures about her, "became available. But nobody had any money," she shrugs, Zen never having been known as a large cash generator. Sure, they needed a place -- but they also needed to pay a $250,000 mortgage. In a fiscal cul-de-sac, one day a $20,000 check came over the proverbial transom. "This is money is sitting around not doing any good," an attached note read. "There's a sense of the great generosity of the universe," Kyoki smiles.

As generous as the universe might be, her daily regimen is nothing if not rugged. Rising every morning for 5:30 *zazen*, Kyoki -- and the small group that joins her in the intimate, wooded Meditation Hall -- engages in silent meditation, generally about the interrelatedness of all beings, followed by 30 minutes of formal chanting in the adjacent Service Hall. "It's a really hard practice," she admits. "But the first time I ever sat, I said, 'I'm home.' Because to sit quietly is such a miraculous thing."

"The mind is one of the senses," she explains. "Instead of seeing, you are thinking. We allow any sense, any emotion to arise. Then we set them aside – we don't think about them. You have to learn how to do this." Kyoki pauses. "We repeat *zazen* at six o'clock in the evening. In the morning," she smiles, "we sit in the dark and let it get light around us."

With up to 30 people coming for *zazen*, Kyoki counts her supporters as roughly 200 -- with a 1,000-person mailing list. Nevertheless, in typical Zen fashion, Kyoki warns that numbers are deceiving. "It's not a creed-based system," she shakes her head. "There's no real joining the Zen Center. People come in, they go out."

What they come for, essentially, are the Zen precepts, Kyoki says, "Do not harm. Do good. Live to benefit all beings. Each action of ours, everything we do, everything we say has a consequence. Because our thoughts, our speech, and our actions have an effect, we have to be very careful about them." Warning that it's not so easy to judge one's life with that sort of micrometer -- while living in the midst of a deeply acquisitive, deeply competitive society -- Kyoki says that "this is an enormous commitment for people. It means taking a leap of faith that is huge."

Yet the environs have been meticulously constructed to aid the Zen pilgrims on their way. Although the log cabin-style house, with its attached two-story farmhouse and nearby barn appear older -- perhaps they're connected to past lives on the land -- they're vintage 1939-59. Strewn with strategically placed statues embodying such traits as perfect wisdom, various bells throughout the house and grounds toll various activities. A fountain tinkles; willows, pines, and rhododendra shade the landscape. On the open-air porch, spider plants and bamboo wind chimes add to a life that is meditative and monastic, contemplative but not necessarily celibate. As a wholly appropriate finishing touch, Kyoki shares her space with birds, bees, and butterflies, all of which flit unfettered about the landscape, and with Mya, the world's friendliest, quietest German Shepherd.

Inside, the Meditation Hall features the Four Vows carved in wood, the Eight-Fold Path above it. Upstairs, a 100-year old Chinese Buddha presides over the Service Hall, a room set aside for bowing and chanting. Hidden during China's murderous Cultural Revolution, a circuitous path found this Buddha a good home in America.

Just as she -- and others -- have found a home in Zen. "Zen Buddhism is a really quiet practice," Kyoki says. "You sit quietly. If I create a me *here*, than I create another *there* in the same instance. But with *zazen* you drop the sense that you are separate from other people and other things. I have to look at you and see that. Then I will understand that kindness is the response when you *don't* see the other person as separate from you.

"The great delusion is separateness," she adds. "And that delusion causes unreasonable amounts of anxiety. People are always trying to re-arrange the world," Kyoki shakes her head. "People are never happy with the way things are. Our emphasis here is getting people to break down that barrier. With *zazen* all separateness drops away. It's the only way I know that does that."

Yes, but even so, for *zazen* acolytes surely there are Spielbergian special effects? Thunder and lightning and fire on the mountain? Earth-shattering revelations on the road to Damascus?

Kyoki smiles patiently. "There aren't big stories in Zen Buddhism," she says. "It's a really quiet practice. At its core, people get to see how *un*exciting this world is."

It even accrues to the Zen Center, Kyoki adds. "You have to hunt us out. There's no proselytizing about it." She gestures about her hilltop aerie. "See how hidden we are?"

CHAPTER FOURTEEN

OLD ST. PATRICK'S CHURCH

It is perhaps the greatest anomaly in all Pittsburgh Houses of Worship: quiet, contemplative St. Patrick's, nearly invisible in the crowded, industrial Strip District, and its boisterous builder, the famous -- some would say infamous -- Father James Cox.

First, the Church, a quiet Irish chapel; a tiny country grotto, contemplative, monastic -- with St. Patrick himself watching over it.

Its lush, walled garden offers a respite from the world -- along with tributes to Our Lady of Lourdes, the Blessed Mother, Saint Bernadette, Saint Ann, Saint Joseph, Saint Patrick, Saint Anthony, and Blessed Kateri Tekawitha -- the Lady of the Mohawks. "The surprising beauty," visitors are told, "reminds us that God's grace can be found in the most unexpected places."

Then there's the creator, Father Cox, one of the most controversial -- and certainly one of the loudest -- Catholic stout, seemingly always fourth incarnation of St. Saint's own day, March 17, worst flood in Pittsburgh A Pittsburgh native born in Cox served the parish from Best remembered outside the in 1932 Father Cox organized on Washington in American  priests in America. Short, shouting, he built this, the Patrick's, to be opened on the 1936 -- coinciding with the history. Lawrenceville in 1886, Father 1923 until his death in 1951. city for his political activism, the largest pre-1960s March history. Leading what came to be known as Cox's Army, Father Cox, himself a veteran of the campaign in France, called for benefits for World War I veterans whom he, and many others, felt had been unfairly denied what was due to them. With a conservatively estimated 25,000 men massed in Washington, living in a tent city, Father Cox & Co. vowed to stay until they got their pensions. With the federal government not about to pay, President Herbert Hoover ended the protest by calling out the army to disperse their fellow former soldiers. The men who led the charge: future World War II commanders Douglas MacArthur and Dwight Eisenhower.

In Pittsburgh, Father Cox had cemented a reputation -- and a role -- for himself as the Pastor of the Poor. In 1929, facing the Great Depression four square, he transformed

his church into an enormous foodbank. Although estimates vary greatly, some say that during Father Cox's 28-
year ministry St. Patrick's served some two million meals -- and handed out 500,000 baskets of food and clothing to the needy.

Although Father Cox has become inalterably linked with his church, St. Patrick's roots run deep into the 19th Century. The oldest Pittsburgh church used devotionally -- Father Harry Nichols
says mass there twice a week, Monday and Thursday afternoons -- it is also the city's first Irish church. Way back in 1808, Father William F.X. O'Brien came to Pittsburgh to establish a parish specifically to see to the needs of a growing Irish population.

Laying a cornerstone at 11th Street and Liberty Avenue that year, Father O'Brien's church was still incomplete when it opened three years later. Unfinished on the inside, too, worshippers had to hire carpenters to make their own pews -- or construct them themselves.

Expanding in 1825, and again in 1826, the Irish ceded the premises to a German congregation in 1834, but moved back in 1840. On August 10, 1854, a Strip District fire burned St. Patrick's to the ground.

Moving three blocks away to 14th Street, the rebuilt St. Patrick's opened on August 15, 1858 -- there to remain, many thought, in perpetuity.

It was not to be. With war and civic expansion intervening, St. Patrick's had to move once again. Losing its site to the Pennsylvania Railroad, St. Patrick's again headed up Liberty Avenue, to 17th Street, the new building opening on December 15, 1865.

More active, more aware, more media savvy, Father Cox arrived in 1923. Within a year, he had re-branded the parish as the American Shrine to Our Lady of Lourdes, a symbol of his own gratitude for a miraculous eye cure he had experienced at the French shrine. The following year, 1925, Father Cox began broadcasting daily mass, a practice he continued for the rest of his life.

And the church building stood, stood for 70 years, until, on March 21, 1935, it burned down -- the second St. Patrick's to suffer such an ignoble fate. A scant year later, a vastly redesigned St. Patrick's -- including a piece of the actual Blarney Stone -- opened in its current location.

Less a parish church (by 1936, the Strip had lost its acres of shanties -- and therefore most of its indigenous population) than a small, two-story devotional chapel, the new St. Patrick's included not only outdoor masses in the beautiful garden grotto, but also a replica of the Holy Stairs in Rome's *Scala Sancta*. (There are other, similar recreations in France, Canada, Lithuania, Italy, and Rhode Island.) Recalling the 28 steps between Christ and Pilate when the Roman Governor said, "Behold the Man" (*Ecce Homo*) and condemned Him to death, the pious ascend them on their knees, saying devotions at each step.

"Dragged on these stairs to be led before Pilate," they say, "I desire to venerate with deep respect the bloodstained traces of Your divine feet."

Such a shrine, such a religious devotion, is unique in the city, highly rare across the world. As such, it is shrouded in mystery: why did Father Cox, a staunch social activist before such things were in vogue, build such a chapel?

Known more for puissance than piety, demonstrations than devotions, what personal needs did he fulfill -- or personal demons exorcise -- by building such a penitential place?

"There was no huge reason to build an Irish church," Father Harry Nichols, the current pastor, shakes his head. "It's almost a devotional chapel," he adds, which is fine -- St. Patrick's is a glorious, enclosed, hermetic, deeply spiritual spot, both inside and out. But in the midst of veterans and labor unrest, in the heart of the Great Depression, where serving meals seemed like St. Patrick's sole mission, such a church seemed the farthest thing from Father Cox's ministry.

Perhaps not. Perhaps for Father Cox the best place to hide was in plain sight. Perhaps the best way for the famous Labor Priest -- who actually ran for President in 1932 on his own Jobless Party ticket -- to indulge in a secret devotion was to do it in his highly unique Irish church. Perhaps it's what he most needed for body and soul and soup kitchens -- a contemplative garden, knee-bound devotional stairs, and a bit of the Blarney Stone to kiss for the gift of eloquence.

An odd, contradictory man, Father Cox; "a strange building," Father Nichols says and shrugs.

CHAPTER FIFTEEN

PITTSBURGH SIKH GURDWARA

When their formal services are over, they sit, in all good fellowship, and partake of healthy vegetarian fare -- all curry and cauliflower -- deliberately so, so that anyone of a mind can join regardless of religious doctrine or dietary restrictions. Open to Sikhs (a Punjabi word meaning a disciple or student), non-Sikhs, and seekers of all stripe, *langar*, this wondrous open meal, is at the heart of Sikh belief -- in a non-sexist, non-racist society where people of all backgrounds are equal, sharing a common meal in the true spirit of unity. Part of *seva*, or community service, another integral part of Sikh practice, *langar* is served in the *gurdwara*, their worship space, and while they don't proselytize, or troll for converts, anyone who wanders in to any *gurdwara* anywhere can join in. "From time to time," offers Sucha Singh, the Pittsburgh Sikh Gurdwara priest, "people come from the universities."

They find their way to a modest suburban street overlooking marked largely by its signature worshippers come to the hear *Shri Guru Granth Sahib*, original Punjabi. Lying beneath opened every morning, closed white brick building on a quiet wooded hillsides, the *gurdwara* gold domes. For their part, Pittsburgh Sikh Gurdwara to the Sikh holy book, read in its a pink and gold coverlet, it is at night.

Often called by the misnomer temple, to which the Sikhs object, feeling that word is better used for Hindu or Buddhist houses of worship, a *gurdwara* is literally their gateway to the guru, their house of study and prayer. Strict monotheists, Sikh worship involves sitting on the floor, in the present case a soft, wall-to-wall carpet. Although in more populous Sikh areas there are religious services all day, every day, here they meet only Sundays, and festival days, for an hour, reading, singing, discoursing, followed by the requisite *langar*.

With a congregation that runs to some 175 families -- from Pennsylvania, Ohio, and West Virignia -- 150 people will gather on any given Sunday, double that for such special occasions as a guru's birthday.

With Pittsburgh Sikh-less for hundreds of years, by the early 1980s some 10 Sikh families, all from India, all physicians and engineers, were meeting monthly, sharing facilities with their fellow Indians – Southern and Northern Hindus and Jains. By mid-decade, the Sikhs founded their own Pittsburgh Sikh Gurdwara and set about creating a building.

Refusing to place a mortgage on the structure, they raised the money among themselves, a half-million dollars. "They made it cash," Singh says.

Not that things were always easy. Going before the Monroeville zoning board, for example, the Sikhs were initially met with opposition, largely due to a concern that the building might sit half-finished forever. After a certain level of wrangling, one Sikh man stood up and said, "I'm donating $100,000 toward this project."

"Then," Singh smiles, "everybody calmed down."

When the building opened in 1985, the congregation gave gift baskets all up and down the street. "Since then," Singh says, "we've had no problems with our neighbors. They like us here." Similarly, when the Pittsburgh Sikh Gurdwara was approached to contribute to a local food pantry, their gifts were substantial. Why not? Singh raises an eyebrow. "We worship for all human beings here."

Although the building was designed by Sikhs, there is nothing symbolic in the architecture, ornamentation, or colorization. The domes, for example, are merely decorative. "They're usually gold," Singh allows, "but sometimes they're white."

Coming in 1992, carrying the title Bhai Sahib Sucha Singh -- which translates roughly as Big Brother, or Knowledgeable Brother -- his priestly duties include being a reader and teacher of Sikh scripture. (By day, he is a Pitt pathology researcher.) His simple sanctuary is a white room, where floral markings are simply pretty, not symbolic, nor is the miniature gold canopy over *Shri Guru Granth Sahib.*

However, in the small altar area there are a sword and shield -- an emblem of Sikhism, symbolic of survival, of self-defense, religious wars being what they are. Although the Sikhs stand today as the world's fifth-most populous religion, with some 26 million followers (most of them in India), nevertheless, they, like many others, have had a troubled and bloody past. "We had to survive," Singh says. "And every individual has to be strong enough to defend his faith." As an example, the last living Sikh guru -- the 10th human guru, who died in the early 18th Century -- had to fight four defensive wars. "You're a saint," Singh says. "But you're a soldier, also."

There is other symbolism in the room. The curvaceous, omnipresent Sikh symbol, *Ek Onkar*, means that there is one God. A large quote in the corner, in Punjabi, reads, "Do not rely on human beings. God gives you everything."

According to the Sikhs, He is manifest through practical living, in serving human beings, and promoting tolerance. While they favor a simple life -- as symbolized in the Sikh prohibition against cutting hair or shaving -- the Sikh gurus did not embrace monasticism or asceticism *per se.* Instead, they taught that any person who makes a living honestly, leads a normal life, and helps the needy can achieve salvation.

Originating with Guru Nanak Dev in the 15th Century, Sikhism follows his and his successors' teaching. In the beginning, the 30-year-old Guru Nanak disappeared for three days. After his return, he proclaimed, "there is neither Hindu nor Muslim. So whose path shall I follow? I shall follow God's path."

Reporting that he had been taken to God's heavenly court and given nectar, Guru Nanak said that he was then commanded, "this is the cup of the adoration of God's name. Drink it. I am with you. I bless you and raise you up. Whoever remembers you will enjoy my favor. Go, rejoice of my name and teach others to do so. I have bestowed the gift of my name upon you. Let this be your calling."

Traveling extensively, teaching his holy wisdom, Guru Nanak inspired many followers. After his death, nine human gurus followed; after them, the guru is *Shri Guru Granth Sahib* itself, codified some 300 years ago. Unique among world scriptures, the Sikhs believe that it, and not any person or assembly, is the Sikh spiritual authority and religious leader. Indeed, as the Sikhs' living guru, *Shri Guru Granth Sahib* is held in great reverence and treated with the utmost respect. As a monotheism, Sikhism rejects idol worship, so *Shri Guru Granth Sahib* is not worshipped as an idol, but rather deeply revered for the ideas that are contained in it -- devotional hymns and poetry which exalt God, stress meditating on God's essence, and dictate moral and ethical rules for developing the soul, achieving salvation, and becoming one with God.

"*Shri Guru Granth Sahib* itself begins," Singh says, "'God is one.' Our religion starts from there."

CHAPTER SIXTEEN

St. Nicholas of Myra Byzantine Catholic Chapel

It was the worst month for mine disasters in American history. In December, 1907, the Monongah Mine explosion, in West Virginia, killed 361 miners; when the Naomi Mine blew up, in Fayette City, it took another 34 lives.
Then came December 19, a cold, dry day along the Youghiogheny River. Although work had been slack, and money short, many Byzantine Catholics living in Jacobs Creek, and environs, refused to go down into the Pittsburgh Coal Company's Darr Mine that day, choosing instead to go to church, there to celebrate the Feast of their Patron, Saint Nicholas, as it was observed on the Julian calendar. (Since 1923, when the Church replaced the Julian calender with the Gregorian, it has been observed on December 6.)
Those who heard the Divine Liturgy were spared -- some say miraculously.

In a mine choked with methane gas and coal regularly blasted with and carried open-flame dirty, dangerous job, in ventilated mines, and the ground regularly courted death.
And death did indeed that morning, as an explosion lay waste to the men and boys -- the single highly flammable dust, miners black powder -- lamps. It was a the dark, poorly men below danger -- and

come at 11:30 enormous mine, killing 239 worst disaster in Pennsylvania mining history. Virtually everyone in the mine was killed -- except the 200 men who instead honored their Patron, Saint Nicholas of Myra.
Their worship -- and their belief in the intercession of Saint Nicholas -- is said to have saved them from a disaster so horrific that most of the bodies were never recovered.
"The Sparing of the Miners," as the event became to be known, simply added to Saint Nicholas's luster, revered as a kind, generous miracle worker. "Our iconographer, Christine Uveges, of Eikona Studios, Cleveland, did the artwork," gestures Fred Petro at the icon on the wall of the Saint Nicholas Byzantine Catholic Chapel, in Beaver. "She

took the story and created this image" -- modern-day miners attending Saint Nicholas' fourth-century funeral. "It is absolutely unique."

So is the chapel that houses it. A wholly wooden church lovingly recreated in Old Country style, it is also the rare house of worship created neither by a congregation nor a church organization, but instead by a fraternal union to honor its own heritage.

Officially the Greek Catholic Union Saint Nicholas Chapel, the GCU -- the country's largest fraternal benefit society serving Byzantine Catholics, the Greek being something of a misnomer -- had discussed building a wooden church for decades, finally erecting it in 1992 for their centenary celebration. Taken directly from the Carpathian style book, those churches in their original Slovakian villages, the chapel stands as three ascending rectangles, each gray-painted wood with white trim, each topped with bulbous domes and crosses. "This was something to honor our fathers," says Petro, who served as project manager.

Painstakingly researching 120 wooden churches from an eight-county region of what was once the Austro-Hungarian Empire, they poured over old maps, records, photographs, even finding some 30 that were still extant. "They survived the Communist era," Petro marvels.

Identifying three styles, they considered a Greek cross (more or less a plus sign), a simple rectangle with a tower, and the one they eventually chose -- three contiguous rectangles progressing upwards at a 30-degree angle. Highly popular in the former counties of Sharish and Zemplin, in what was known as SubCarpathian Rus, Saint Nicholas Chapel's pedigree is exacting: the tower from the Church of the Blessed Virgin Mary in Mikulasova (Sharish County), later relocated to the open air museum in Bardejov; the center from the Church of St. Michael the Archangel in Nova Sedlica (Zemplin County); and the altar from the Church of St. Nicholas in Zboj (Zemplin County).

Asking a retired draftsman to make a couple of renderings, the GCU retained Thomas Stephen Terpack, a Point Breeze architect, to draw up the plans. "We built the chapel to have the look of antiquity," Petro says, "but with modern conveniences" -- including climate control, rest facilities, and a lower-level museum containing artifacts from the GCU, the Byzantine Catholic Church, and Carpatho-Rusyn history.

With oak and yellow pine interiors, and a cedar exterior, the 70-seat sanctuary is quiet, contemplative. "If I would use one word to describe our chapel," Petro says, "it would be 'prayerful.'"

As part of that atmosphere, of an open conversation with God, Petro points out that the church does not have a spire penetrating heaven; instead, he says, the domes -- especially the central dome, containing an icon of Christ -- indicate "that the Heavens are open and God is with us."

Inside the altar, separated from the sanctuary by an icon screen, Mary is shown with her Son. "In the Eastern Rite," Petro says, "Mary is never depicted alone, but always with Christ. Heaven and Earth could not contain the presence of God, but somehow He is contained in her womb. Therefore, Mary represents the unity of Heaven and Earth, of God and Human."

A unique feature of this chapel is that the side walls contain 10 icons displaying the life of Saint Nicholas -- instead, say, of the life of Christ or the Stations of the Cross. Painted in the Byzantine style, "the iconographs are not meant to look real," Petro says, "but instead to depict the inner meaning, the spirituality of the event."

Following the biography of their Patron, the icons illustrate Saint Nicholas' birth and baptism in Myra (in modern Turkey); the day he was taken to his uncle Nicholas, Bishop of Patara, for his Christian education; his gift of three bags of gold coins for the dowries of a poor man's three daughters; his ordination as a bishop; his death (attended by the Jacobs Creek miners); and his posthumous miracles -- safely returning a kidnapped child; as the patron of seamen, saving a boatload of sailors from drowning; insuring that a ship full of grain arrived in Myra; staying the executioner's sword above three men unjustly condemned to death; and appearing to Emperor Constantine in a dream.

Three years after the chapel was built, in 1995 Metropolitan Archbishop Judson Procyk designated it as a parish of the Archeparchy, appointing Archpriest John G. Petro -- Fred's brother -- as pastor. While so consecrating the chapel did not replace any existing church, a small but enthusiastic community flocked to the new worship space.

Hosting regular services, baptisms, and funerals, "Saint Nicholas functions as any other parish would," Father Petro says, "and there are people who do indeed count this as their parish."

As well they should, for Saint Nicholas really celebrates two local miracles. The first, of course, is the 200 lives saved on December 19, 1907. The second, more recent, is that after building their gem of a chapel, everyone remained friends. In fact, to celebrate its completion, they all enjoyed a dinner together. "If we had everything to do again," Fred Petro says proudly, "we'd do it the same way."

CHAPTER SEVENTEEN

St. Anthony's Chapel

It must have been something to see, trolleys hauling the lame and the halt by the hundreds, up impossibly steep Troy Hill, there to be healed by the holy relics housed in St. Anthony's Chapel.

Although reliable numbers are impossible to ascertain, it may be that St. Anthony's contains the world's largest collection of authenticated relics -- some 5,000 saints' and martyrs' bones, clothing, possessions -- all in altars, boxes, glass cases; all presumed to have the power to hear, to help, to heal. "There's an old saying," offers Carole Brueckner, the Chapel's lay president, "that a dead saint is better than a live physician."

Built by a Belgian in a German neighborhood to honor an Italian -- at a time when America was calling itself the great Melting Pot -- St. Anthony's Chapel remains no more probable today than when it was opened more than a century ago. Indeed, asks Brueckner, "where would you find a place like this other than in Europe?"

Logic might dictate that it should never have been built in the first place.

The story begins in 1868, when Father Suitbertas Gottfried Mollinger, a 40-year-old priest as well as a scion of a wealthy Belgian family, was named pastor of the Most Holy Name of Jesus Parish, Troy Hill's Catholic Church. While stationed in America, Father Mollinger maintained strong ties with Europe, and, in an era of Garibaldi and Bismarck, when revolution was sweeping across the continent, the ill winds were blowing relics out of their monasteries, grottos, and shrines -- and into pawnshops and onto the black market.

While church law does not permit trafficking in relics *per se*, Father Mollinger bought everything he could, bringing them to these shores for safe-keeping. Then, to house his treasures, he used $300,000 of his own money to commission a private chapel based on the European model of the Chapel Royale. Literally state-of-the-art when it opened in 1883, St. Anthony's is figured in exquisite craftsmanship, literally priceless today, imported largely from Germany and Italy. Although it is believed that Father Mollinger kept scrupulous records of his art, even of the artisans themselves, many papers were destroyed in a subsequent fire. "It's difficult to get information," Brueckner says. "There are some things we just don't know."

Dedicating his private shrine to St. Anthony of Padua, Father Mollinger stocked it with bone fragments and clothing swatches, as well as such holy objects as a splinter from the

True Cross, a thorn from the Crown of Thorns, and a piece of stone from the Holy Sepulcher. In addition, there are relics of all 12 Apostles, a tooth from St. Anthony himself (the only known relic outside of Padua), St. Demetrius' entire body in a golden sarcophagus, the skull of St. Theodore, and so on, all carefully catalogued so that the faithful can go to exact spot and direct to their devotions. "It's so unique," Brueckner says.

So is the riddle at the heart of St. Anthony's: why Father Mollinger felt so attached to this Paduan saint. Whether it was in gratitude for something the famed Wonder Worker had done for his family, or in supplication for continued maintenance of a beloved family member or friend, it's another fact lost in history. "Perhaps," Brueckner shrugs, "he had a special devotion."

Regardless of reason, devoted Father Mollinger certainly was -- and his devotion drew thousands. In its heyday, St. Anthony's attracted pilgrims from all over the world to experience the relics' remarkable curative powers. With the streetcar that brought the faithful up Troy Hill dubbed "the ambulance" because of whom it carried, some 3,000 reportedly walked away without their canes or crutches -- or eyeglasses. To this day, the Chapel has affidavits on file from people who came and were cured. "There are miracles that we see every day," Brueckner says.

Still, it's no longer the same as it once was. In the old days, the little village of Troy Hill became so crowded around St. Anthony's Day, June 13, that residents rented out rooms, porches, even chairs for pilgrims to sleep on.

As Father Mollinger's remarkable collection increased, including 14 life-sized, anatomically correct wood carvings of the Stations of the Cross (fashioned by artists at the royal Ecclesiastical Art Establishment of Mayer and Company in Munich, and said to be a true global one-of-a-kind), Father Mollinger -- a full six feet tall, a robust 300 pounds, and sporting a waist-length white beard -- planned an addition, itself adorned with 14 stained glass windows honoring the Apostles, Saint Paul, the Holy Mother, and others.

On dedication day, 1892, Father Mollinger collapsed, then died two days later. Since Father Mollinger personally owned the chapel, and left no will, Pittsburgh's Bishop Richard Phelan, acting as trustee for the parish, bought the Chapel from Father Mollinger's heirs and re-sold it to the parish. "The people of Most Holy Name of Jesus Parish are the caretakers of St. Anthony's Chapel," Brueckner says.

But times and religious practices change, and St. Anthony's faded, due in part to water damage and general disuse. In an effort spearheaded by legendary Troy Hill activist Mary Wohleber, the neighborhood raised some $250,000 to restore the Chapel to its original splendor (plus updated lighting, air conditioning, and alarm systems.) "The

Chapel would probably not be here if it were not for her persistence and her dedication," Brueckner says.

Although in times past, as a private, devotional chapel and not a church, St. Anthony's did not have regularly scheduled masses, due to the Chapel's continued popularity a Tuesday morning mass has been instituted. Today, it draws some 75 people – that number swelling to 200 during spring Holy season.

Aside from mass, the Chapel attracts thousands of visitors from all over the world. "People come from everywhere," Brueckner says, Africa to Australia, Israel to Ireland to Italy, not only tourists coming to see the curios, the gold and jewels, the statues and skulls, but also the pious pursuing private devotions, devout Catholics like Art Rooney and Imelda Marcos. While Brueckner is certain there have been many more celebrities

who have visited, given the Chapel's private nature "people don't tell us who they are," she says.

To add to the St. Anthony's experience, for the first time in its history the Chapel offers tours, sells DVDs and a glossy illustrated history, even operates a gift shop. "Anyone is welcome," Brueckner says. "Most definitely."

All the history aside, the swirl of color and stunning visual splendor, Brueckner believes St. Anthony's biggest draw is that it's quiet and tranquil, deliberately so. "It's a true religious experience," she says. A place of solace, of meditation and private prayer, "it's my little bit of heaven here on earth," Brueckner adds. "Everybody needs peace of mind." She pauses. "Peace of soul."

CHAPTER EIGHTEEN

St. Nicholas Croatian Catholic Church

Maxo Vanka was an artist with talent to burn -- and an ax to grind.

Deeply conflicted about his Catholicism, in the face of global conflagration he was passionately pacifist -- and a committed anti-capitalist. With all the burning power of art, he transformed Millvale's St. Nicholas Croatian Catholic Church into the testimony of his creed.

While it seems an odd place for polemics, given the church's quiet, working-class congregation, Vanka used it as his personal bully pulpit -- and for his own journey of religious discovery.

First, the canvas. Coming to Pittsburgh between 1880-1920, the Croatians, largely finding work in the mills and mines, formed a parish on the North Side, 1894. Five years later, under the leadership of Father Franjo Glojnaric, and literally using their own pocket change, they purchased part of what was then called Bennett Hill from William J. Mellon for $7,500. Reviewing the plans for their new $24,000 church, the 102 forward-thinking parishioners agreed that it must have central heating and electric lights -- the latter idea a bold step in an area that at the time was not yet electrified.

Dedicated on May 15, 1900, the 550-seat Romanesque St. Nicholas Croatian Catholic Church celebrated its first mass six months later, replete with a $2,000 organ, a gift from Mr. Andrew Carnegie.

There matters might have stood for a century or more until two a.m., March 26, 1921, when a fire destroyed the church -- burned everything, in fact, except for a statue of the Virgin Mary, which stood steadfast at the altar. Fourteen months later, May 30, 1922, they dedicated the replacement.

A decade later they had a new pastor. A native Croatian, Father Albert Zagar came to America in 1927; by 1932 he was the spiritual leader of St. Nicholas. After looking at the church's bare walls for five years, in 1937 he was ready to paint them. But with what?

Enter the artist. A friend suggested that Father Zagar look into a skilled muralist -- and admitted agnostic -- named Maxo Vanka, who had emigrated to America in 1934. Coming to Millvale, Vanka saw enormous potential in the intimate space. The deal was struck: as long as he presented traditional religious themes, Father Zagar gave Vanka a

free hand. In the end, his work made him immortal -- and the Millvale church world famous.

Instructed to "paint what you want," Vanka did just that, alpha to omega, fiery angelology to fearsome demonology, tirades against war and capitalism, the Four Gospels, Old Testament homilies, Crucifictions, Ascensions, and more. Here, a World War I doughboy inflicts the crucified Jesus' fatal wound. There, a Johnstown mine explosion frames the exhumation of the dead. All around, mothers weep over the dying and departed.

Painting virtually non-stop, his daughter Peggy Vanka Brasko wrote that "my father worked at painting the murals at a furious pace. He usually worked between 16 to 18 hours daily through the entire week."

Starting in early April, 1937, the 47-year-old Vanka worked alone, generally until two in the morning, finishing the main body of work on June 10. Returning four years later, in 1941, he added such murals as Mother Croatia on the Cross; an Old Testament wall, including such repeated Vanka themes as Thou Shalt Not Kill and the Golden Calf; a New Testament wall, including the Eye of God, the Resurrection, and St. Peter with Keys to the Kingdom.

Mary Petrich, now a St. Nicholas tour guide, was born and baptised in the church, as was her mother. Remembering Father Zagar as a humble, highly intelligent man, a Franciscan whose worn shoes were stuffed with cardboard, she recalls him combing the parish to collect money, then blessing people's houses in the name of the Three Kings. "He was a good man," she smiles.

As a schoolgirl, she and others often came to visit the church when Vanka was painting -- and came away frightened by his troubling, extremely graphic renderings of war and death.

They're there in abundance. Hardly designed to comfort troubled souls, Vanka's lurid murals, which cover virtually the entire church interior, present his own tortured view of mankind. One mural, for example, draws the direct comparison between the Holy Mother crying at the Crucifixion, a Croatian mother shedding tears as she raises her sons for war, and an immigrant mother distraught as she sends her sons to industry.

The figure of Injustice, wearing a ghastly gas mask, is figured with unequal scales and a bloody sword. Prudence is a World War I ambulance driver. An angry Mary tries to stop soldiers from killing each other.

St. Nicholas is full of such images -- and stark dichotomies. Populated by the saved and the lost, the redeemed and the damned, Vanka depicts the generosity of the poor as they share a simple meal, while a rich man -- waited on by black servants, ignoring an amputee begging at his feet -- eats alone.

All told, Mary Petrich says, "these murals are challenging."

Nevertheless, they are not without whimsy or nostalgia. While Old Country peasants kneel and pray to Mary beneath a traditional hilltop church, a flock of decidedly non-Croatian turkeys strolls by. Perhaps through painting a plethora of religious visions, Vanka himself 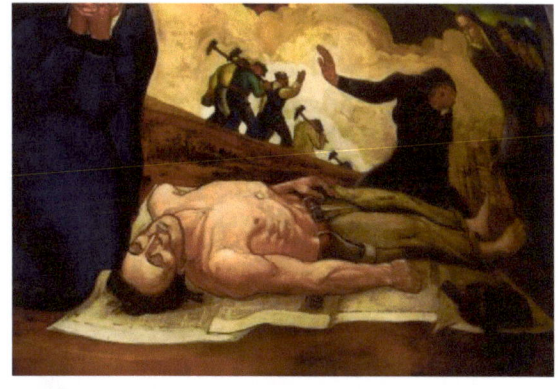 made peace with his own Catholic heritage. As many artists have, Vanka painted himself into some scenes, a Croatian farm hand here, an apostle there, gazing at Christ's ascension into Heaven.

After completing his masterpiece, Vanka said that "these murals are my contribution to America -- not only mine, but my immigrant people's, who are grateful, like me, that they are not in the slaughter of Europe."

Perhaps, then, his most profound legacy is not the horrific images but instead the power of gratitude and of prayer. Central to St. Nicholas is the large altar painting of the Mother and Child, in regal trappings and traditional Croatian colors, bearing the inscription, *Marijo, Kralijce Hrvatska, mol za nas*! (Mary, Queen of Croatians, Pray for us!)

For all of Vanka's nightmares, that is the feeling that fills the church. Once known for singing in Croatian -- so passionately that they feared for the windows -- it is that way no longer. "It was a happy parish," docent Rose Augustine recalls. Baptized, confirmed, and married here, Augustine also married off three daughters and a son at St. Nicholas. "I loved coming to church," she says.

She still does, although they celebrate the traditional Croatian Mass only the second Sunday of every month. In addition, the adjacent school closed some 20 years ago, the parish house stands empty, and only 180 of the 500 seats are regularly filled for mass. While many descendents of the original Croatian founders may have moved away -- to Shaler, the North Hills, and beyond -- still, Rose Augustine says, St. Nicholas "is like a little family."

No time more than at Christmas, when people pour back into the church, all the children wearing traditional Croatian dress. "It's beautiful," Mary Petrich says. "It really is."

CHAPTER NINETEEN

MACEDONIA CHURCH OF PITTSBURGH

"What do you *do* when you need a miracle?" the Reverend Jason Barr calls out, imploring his congregants to think along with him. Anecdotal, approachable, above all human, his sermon is punctuated by organ and bass, tambourine and piano -- and by people nodding, raising their hands, muttering assent, rising as witnesses -- at the crescendo, jumping up to applaud.

"When you *need* a miracle," he gestures, "you admit your need for help. You focus on God and *not* the problem. That's where we flunk, right there."

He has drawn a few hundred people this sunny Sunday morning, to the predominantly African-American Macedonia Church on Bedford Avenue, and he's determined to help them out of the hole we're in.

"The older I get," Reverend Barr continues, "the more I learn how to just leave it in the Lord's hands. When God is *your* co-pilot, you crash the plane. I don't need *Him* to be my co-pilot. I need Him to be my pilot. I need Him to give me direction. To tell me where to go. To tell me what to do. To keep me out of some of the mess that I've been in.

"When you get in a difficult situation, you say, 'Lord, I thank you for the answer -- *in advance*. I thank you for deliverance -- *in advance*. I thank you for the blessing -- *in advance*."

The air in Macedonia -- so named because in *Acts* Paul is called there to preach -- is an anomaly, charged, crackling with life-changing messages, yet decidedly casual. With a jazz combo ever-present during the entire service, making it seem more Saturday night than Sunday morning, the message nevertheless is Salvation, as in many houses of worship, layered over with a large dollop of personal pride and individual responsibility. This is all done less for entertainment than for a religious purpose. Coming in 1988, Reverend Barr found a moribund congregation that hadn't changed in decades. "We literally unlocked the doors," Reverend Barr says. "The church had become a fortress rather than a sanctuary. I said, 'we're a church not just for the select few.' We became more open and accepting. And we grew."

Feeling that Macedonia was spinning its wheels using old-fashioned Eurocentric liturgies -- "we were bound to a culture and tradition that did not do well," he recalls --

Reverend Barr had added a little spice and soul into the services – not to mention keyboards, guitars, traps, and congas. Attendance, which had been hovering at a weekly 300, more than quintupled to 1,600 -- and membership skyrocketed to 3,000. Now the largest congregation in the Hill, and third-largest African-American congregation in Pittsburgh, "at Macedonia," Reverend Barr says, "they take *pride* in being African-American."

It was always that way. Founded in 1903 as Macedonia Baptist Church, all 12 members worshipped in a two-room house. By the 1920s, the congregation had grown into its own signature Bedford Avenue facility -- one designed by Pennsylvania's first black woman architect. Completely financed and constructed by African-Americans, from the inlaid wood ceiling to the stained glass windows, the congregation reveled in their hand-hewn home. And they wouldn't leave: in 1940, the City of Pittsburgh asked Macedonia to relocate to the nearby corner lot so that a new recreation center could be erected on their site. The congregation abjectly refused. "No matter how much land the City promised them," Reverend Barr says, "they wouldn't go. They were so proud of what they had done."

By 1944, the church boasted 1,600 members, and while it experienced a decline in the '60s, these days Macedonia has dramatically expanded its reach to include such vital social service programs as the Macedonia Family and Community Enrichment Center (Macedonia FACE), which operates the Family Group Decision making program, HIV and AIDs education, the Macedonia Counseling Center, Freedom School, Ammon Recreation Center, and other social service programs.

Becoming a place to see and be seen, former Steeler J.T. Thomas is a member (as was Kordell Stewart), as were former City Councilman and School Board president Jake Milliones (whose SRO funeral was held in Macedonia in 1993), jazz great Stanley Turrentine, and Hall of Fame Negro League home-run king Josh Gibson.

Speaking of stars, the likes of singer Etta Cox and trumpet maestro Wynton Marsalis have been known to show up for matins; sometimes, the jazz gets so hot that 900 people have packed into the sanctuary, sitting on stairs and folding chairs in addition to the pews.

Although the main sanctuary comfortably holds 750, it looks smaller. The feeling, Revered Barr says, is one of "intimacy. You're very connected to everything going on. Macedonia," he adds, "is the kind of place where everybody knows when you're there and when you're not."

A lot of *there* runs to Sunday mornings, when Reverend Barr conducts three separate services -- and, he admits, "it's a challenge to develop a message for all three."

The 8:00 A.M. flavor is for older people, generally over 60.

The 10:00 A.M. version is for middle-aged folks, 40-60.

Then, at 12:00 P.M. comes the under-35 crowd -- which often starts at 50 people, only to swell tenfold by service's end. "That's our seeker service," he says. "They're searching. They're not connected to each other or to the church. But they're here. And they're seeking."

Yes, but preaching to the not-yet-churched often leads to amusing incidents involving people who, not brought up in an ecclisiastic persuasion, and not understanding church decorum, don't quite know the moves. For example, Reverend Barr says, "they bring refreshments. They bring a cooler. They're ready to picnic."

That's in church, during services. Like the time one woman came on Sunday with a passel of kids, plopped herself down in a pew, and proceeded to open up a bucket of Kentucky Fried and passed out the finger-lickin'.

Then there are those wandering souls who take the rich Baptist tradition of call-and-response a little too liberally. Like the fellow who, infused with the spirit of witnessing, shouted out during Pastor Barr's sermon, "say it, motherfucker! That motherfucker is *saying* something!"

Hm.

After services, Pastor Barr took the man aside and said, "ah, Brother, thank you for your support and encouragement. But in church – in *my* church – we usually answer in a different way. Next time the spirit so strikes, please try saying *Amen*."

Finally, there was the woman who, chagrined at her children's behavior, started beating them *in situ*. (She, too, was gently told, 'Sister, there's a time and place…')

"They are seriously seeking to do better," Reverend Barr says. "For the most part, they want a better life. Whosoever will," he adds, "let them come. And they're coming just the way they are. In turn, I have to come at the message in a completely different way."

Reverend Barr gazes out at his sanctuary. "Twenty-one years ago there was not a lot of noise in Macedonia," he shakes his head. "Now it's a *vibrant* kind of worship."

CHAPTER TWENTY

St. Nicholas Orthodox Church

Our story begins, harrowingly enough, in the McKees Rocks Bottoms, turn of the previous century. Seems that there was a growing community of immigrants from the East -- Russians, Carpatho-Rusyns, Ukrainians, Galicianers -- who, naturally enough, wanted to go to church, *their* church, on Sundays and Feast Days. However, the closest house of worship with their liturgy and lingo was Saint Alexander Nevsky, then in Allegheny (now in Allison Park.) At that time, the only way across the Ohio River was by boat. So by boat -- some rowboats, some little more than skiffs -- they went, in all weathers, in all stages of river rise, all before the Army Corps of Engineers tamed the waters.

Beginning in roughly 1905, and for a decade after, they made their dangerous pilgrimage across the waters, now shallow and still, now swift and swollen, their small boats jouncing back and forth. Finally, in 1914, with a critical mass of 120 families, they formed their own congregation, St. Nicholas Orthodox Church. Meeting in Serbian Hall, collecting money for a building, "they had a rough go of it," says Father Thomas Soroka, the current rector and the son and grandson of former rectors. (It is widely believed that St. Nicholas is the lone Orthodox Church in America to have such a trio as rectors. Alas, the line stops there: Father Soroka is the proud papa of three lovely daughters.) Digging into their newly purchased plot on Munson Avenue, pouring a foundation, they prayed in the basement for the better part of two years, 1915-17, until they were able to finish what was then a fairly Spartan church -- no electricity, no rest facilities, no pews (that, at least, was the traditional Orthodox style; seats came 20-odd years later), neither icons nor images. But it was Russian, and it was Orthodox, and it had a half-dozen gold domes topped with Byzantine crosses. "There's an openness here," Father Soroka says, "a warmth, an intimacy. The people are very proud of it."

When the icons and images came, they were a decided hodge-podge. Beginning in summer 1941 the project to paint the walls and ceiling was headed by W. Naidenoff, an art teacher, noted Pittsburgh theater decorator, and man who never seemed to use his first name. "He used the church as a training ground for students," Father Soroka shrugs. "At the time, it was the best that they could do."

Hardly completed in the traditional Byzantine style, the western-style paintings are highly "uneven," he says. Some are rather good -- telling, evocative; others are flat and amateurish. A third group are outright copies of the Dutch Masters' re-telling of biblical scenes -- without the originals' color, style, or panache.

On the altar, the iconostasis, painted by a congregant named Constantine Kosak, is clearly in a western not Byzantine mode. In many cases, the traditional colorations or poses are incorrect -- meaning that they are paintings, or representations, and not true icons. To top it off, in the Byzantine rite, God is *never* figured; nevertheless, there He is, above it all, appearing suitably patriarchal.

Predictably, one current church faction prefers the more traditional approach and wants all the questionable icons replaced. Another group loves the old images, wants them retained. "It's a very sensitive thing," Father Soroka says. "From a theological standpoint, I know it's wrong. From a practical standpoint, I have to tread very lightly."

One treasure that everyone agrees on is in the front of the church, a small reliquary, containing likenesses and tiny bone fragments of Saint Herman, Saint Innocent, and Saint Tikhon, all involved in the Russian church, all linked to America. Having the relics here is "considered a great blessing," Father Soroka says. "It is considered a sign of God's presence working in the life of that saint.

"Orthodoxy is always a living connection with the past," he adds.

That connection resulted in slow but steady growth through the Great Depression and World War II; after 1945, the baby and industrial boom caused membership to spike sevenfold. At St. Nicholas, part of the surge was due to good economic times, part to

the charismatic Father Alexander Varlashkin, who served 45 years, 1931-76. A greatly revered rector who is still remembered fondly today, "he was really beloved," Father Soroka says.

After Father Varlashkin's departure, though, St. Nicholas faced a double whammy -- the people's changing culture and the area's spectacular economic collapse.

Sixty years ago, the congregants enjoyed Russian language and culture in their homes. After World War II, as Americanization (and intermarriage) took root, and the Red Scare rattled people's ethnic identities, Eastern culture began to evaporate. "People downplayed being Russian," Father Soroka says. For the first time, they brought an American flag into church, where it still stands. Nevertheless, the stop-gaps didn't help. "We experienced a tremendous decline," he adds.

It got so bad that hardly unique is the story Father Soroka tells of a funeral at which he officiated not so long ago. Your central casting Russian grandmother -- a bubba, a babushka -- passed on, and 110 people -- family, friends, beloved fellow travelers -- came to St. Nicholas to pay their respects. "Not one of them was an Orthodox Christian," Father Soroka raises a finger. "Not one."

To make matters worse, as Pittsburgh was badly served in the disastrous 1980s, McKees Rocks was the regional bellwether. As thousands departed, even the church debated relocating -- albeit close by, in Kennedy Township, but nevertheless giving up its traditional home. Ultimately deciding to tough it out, "here," he gestures, "they were extremely visible. Here, they were easily accessible. We've grown for that."

Indeed, St. Nicholas has had a miraculous rebirth of sorts. "Today," he says, "Orthodoxy is a religion for everyone. We've been rather successful attracting non-Orthodox people. People come looking for depth, a sense of rootedness, a sense of history." For their part, the passionate newcomers to Orthodoxy want a return to more traditional forms and functions. They would love to see the pews torn out, the walls and icon screen scrubbed clean and repainted in the traditional figurations. "It's an incredible irony," Father Soroka says. "The people who were given the Orthodox faith as a gift are happy with the way things

have been. The converts want a return to tradition. To try to get them all to sing from the same hymn book is tricky. It requires a tremendous amount of patience. And love." He calls his flock a tapestry, which seems very much to the point. At Pascha -- their version of Easter -- they read the Gospel in a 12 languages, including English, Slovanic, Russian, Arabic, Ukrainian, Aramaic, German, Greek, Japanese, and French. "When the traditional Russian culture goes away," he says, "all you have left is the faith. That's where our church is right now. We're in flux. A century later, we're beginning again. We're starting over." He pauses. "We have to do that."

CHAPTER TWENTY-ONE

RODEF SHALOM CONGREGATION

Here's a workable definition of clout -- the first American synagogue sufficiently powerful to entice a sitting President to give a short but salient speech on tolerance and religious pluralism during Sabbath morning services. In this case, it was Rodef Shalom Congregation, whose name means Pursuer of Peace, and whose charismatic leader, Rabbi J. Leonard Levy, had personally pursued President William Howard Taft to visit, Saturday, May 29, 1909.

Standing before the packed house -- 900 on the floor, another 300 in the balcony -- America's all-time most corpulent Chief Executive gazed out on some of Pittsburgh's most prominent citizens, including the mercantile magnate Kaufmann brothers and Barney Dreyfuss, the future Hall-of-Fame Pirates owner who invented the World Series as a showcase for his National League Champions, and quipped, "my friends, I do not claim to conform very strictly to religious observances, but it has remained for the city of Pittsburgh to bring me to church both on Saturday and on Sunday." After the chuckling died down, Taft added that "I esteem it a great privilege to appear before this intelligent  and patriotic audience at the insistence of your leader. The prayer to which we have just listened, full of liberality and kindness and humanity, makes one feel ashamed of all narrowness and bigotry in religion, and it makes me glad to say that never in the history of the country...have the Jewish people failed to live up to the highest standard of citizenship and of patriotism."

Summoning all his national pride, Mr. Taft added how happy he was that "the Constitutional provision that there shall be no religious requirements under any circumstances for any office or citizenship in this country is evidenced by a President of these United States in a Jewish tabernacle, where he may feel as much at home as if he were in any other church."

Then, during the singing of "America," he left, to dedicate Arsenal Park's new fountain, and to see a Pirate game at Mr. Dreyfuss' newfangled Forbes Field, America's first poured concrete baseball park, that looked out at Mr. Carnegie's Institute and Mrs. Schenley's Park.

Although it had been a long time coming, Rodef Shalom had arrived. Some 62 years prior, in 1847, 12 German-Jewish emigrées had established a Jewish burial society, Bais Almon (Mourners' House), buying land on Troy Hill for a cemetery. The following year, 1848, they rented a room at Penn Avenue and Sixth Street, Downtown, calling themselves Shaare Shemayim (Gate of Heaven) Congregation.

As the group settled down to make a home in America, synagogue life was often turbulent. Four years later, in 1852, a group formed a breakaway congregation -- that lasted but a year before returning. Sadly, the marriage wasn't a happy one, and a scant two years later, in 1855, another group departed, forming what is now Rodef Shalom Congregation. Chartered by the Commonwealth the following year, 1856, Rodef Shalom re-merged with former rival Shaare Shemayim in 1860 to form a robust 35-family synagogue.

Using a rented hall on St. Clair Street in Allegheny, then the region's Jewish center, by 1861 they began construction their own building, back across the Allegheny River, at Hancock Street (now Eighth Street) and Penn Avenue, Downtown. Befitting the dual nature of the group, the worship services were all in Hebrew -- but the clergy dressed German-style, while their sermons did double duty in German and English.

While Rodef Shalom was strictly Orthodox, after an 1863 visit by the charismatic Rabbi Isaac Mayer Wise, a founder of the new Reform movement, a majority of the congregants voted to adopt the new customs. Predictably, the minority who preferred the traditional liturgy upped and left, moving across town to form the then-Orthodox Tree of Life Synagogue. (Outgrowing Downtown, Tree of Life moved to Oakland, in buildings that became the Pittsburgh Playhouse, finally to Squirrel Hill, at Wilkins and Shady Avenues.)

A major congregation needs a major leader, and at the century's turn Rodef Shalom hired Rabbi J. Leonard Levy, the dynamic man they needed to take their great leap forward. Serving 1901-17, Rabbi Levy came at a time of vastly increased immigration -- and vastly increased fortunes. Tripling in size from 1901 to 1908, for example, Rodef Shalom's increasingly wealthy members were on the move -- from Allegheny and the Hill District to Oakland, Shadyside, and East Liberty.

Arriving just in time for the dedication of a second building on the same Downtown site, Rabbi Levy spearheaded the move east. Choosing Oakland, the city's emerging Civic Center, Rodef Shalom paid $60,000 for a lot at Morewood and Fifth Avenues; what stands today as Pittsburgh's grandest synagogue cost $250,000 more.

At the time, Henry Hornbostel was Pittsburgh's premier architect, the man whom Andrew Carnegie selected to design his Institute of Technology (now Carnegie-Mellon University). Winning the design competition for the new Rodef Shalom, for the exteriors Hornbostel specified yellow brick with terra cotta decorations. In the grand sanctuary, his 90-foot masonry dome (with its stained glass skylight) was America's largest. In addition, the worship space incorporated four enormous William Willet stained glass windows -- Moses interceding for the Jewish people, as well as with individuals performing acts of kindness, including tending the sick and feeding the poor. The *pièce-de-résistance* was a Kimball organ, at the time the third-largest in the world. "It's huge," Executive Director Jeff Herzog gestures. "It's old. It still plays."

If Hornbostel's masterpiece, which opened in 1907, accomplished nothing else, it clearly announced that these Pittsburgh Jews had made it. This was not a small, European-style synagogue, no drab house of worship hidden on a side street. Instead, it took its rightful place on Fifth Avenue, in the middle of Millionaires Row, cheek-to-jowl with St. Paul Cathedral.

With significant additions to the building 30 and 50 years later, and major renovations in 1990 and 2000, Rodef Shalom includes two intimate auxiliary sanctuaries, a 10,000-volume library, and the Wechsler Gallery, a circular room containing priceless *objects d'art*, some dating back thousands of years.

In terms of dating back, Rodef Shalom's deep roots continue to bear fruit. Some families are 8th-generation members; Herzog himself is fourth, his son fifth. While at its zenith, roughly a half-century ago, Rodef Shalom boasted some 2,300 families, these days that number has dropped to roughly 1,100 – still making it Pennsylvania's largest Reform congregation.

There is an interesting and unique coda to all this architectural *sturm und drang*. Literally returning to Judaism's agricultural roots, in 1987 Rodef Shalom's Dr. Walter Jacob, who fled to America after watching his family's Augsburg synagogue burn on *Krystallnacht*, November 9-10, 1938, created America's sole Biblical garden on the temple's grounds. Growing plants which are exclusively mentioned in the Bible, he has samples of barley, wheat, dates, figs, pomegranates -- some 100 different species in all, each labeled with its biblical reference.

Come out early, June through September, at, say, six in the morning. You'll find him there, standing in the shade of Pittsburgh's grandest Temple, a gentle, decent man, Holocaust survivor and Rabbi Emeritus, tending his garden.

CHAPTER TWENTY-TWO

ST. PAUL CATHEDRAL

It had not been an easy decision. Bishop Richard Phelan cast his cold churchman's eye about his Downtown cathedral and knew the future was rising against him -- literally. He had long ago parted company with the medieval notion that the church spires must stand as the town's zenith -- that, he understood, was for a simpler, less compacted, less vertical age. Now, at century's turn, he knew that Pittsburgh's new steel-skeletoned buildings, and nascent mechanical elevators, meant the eclipse of his twin spires -- Christ and His Mother -- at the corner of Fifth Avenue and Grant Street. Besides, he shrugged heavily, it had been more than a decade since his Saint Paul Cathedral had been -- if not dwarfed, then at least had its rightful position usurped by Henry Hobson Richardson's new Courthouse -- Allegheny County's secular temple of justice catercorner across Grant Street. A pragmatist as well as a visionary, Bishop Phelan understood the central political issue: who could successfully argue with that?

His church needed more room, and, with a rising debt, needed more money as well. Nevertheless, to stay put meant losing stature daily -- as ever-higher buildings were erected. In addition, as fewer and fewer people lived in the heart of the city, the Bishop ran the risk of having a perpetually empty cathedral. With no parish, no flock to tend, his cathedral would stand open only for special diocesan occasions. No, that could never be.

With Pittsburgh brawny and bustling, and Downtown real estate commanding premium prices, it was time to render unto Caesar -- or Mammon -- what was his, put his ledgers in the black, and move the cathedral to more fertile ground.

Taking a bold step, Bishop Phelan commanded that the cathedral be torn down. Selling the land to Henry Clay Frick for $1.325 million -- at the time the most lucrative real estate transaction in Pittsburgh history -- Bishop Phelan moved St. Paul Cathedral to Oakland, a burgeoning suburb a half-dozen miles east. (For his part, Mr. Frick replaced the downtown church with his highly ornamental Union Arcade.)

Still, in 1903, when the Cathedral's cornerstone was laid on Fifth Avenue, Oakland was barely on Pittsburgh's cultural map. The Pirates, for example, playing in Allegheny, in Exposition Park, were a half-dozen years away from their own signature facility, Forbes Field. The University of Pittsburgh, also on the North Side, was similarly six years from

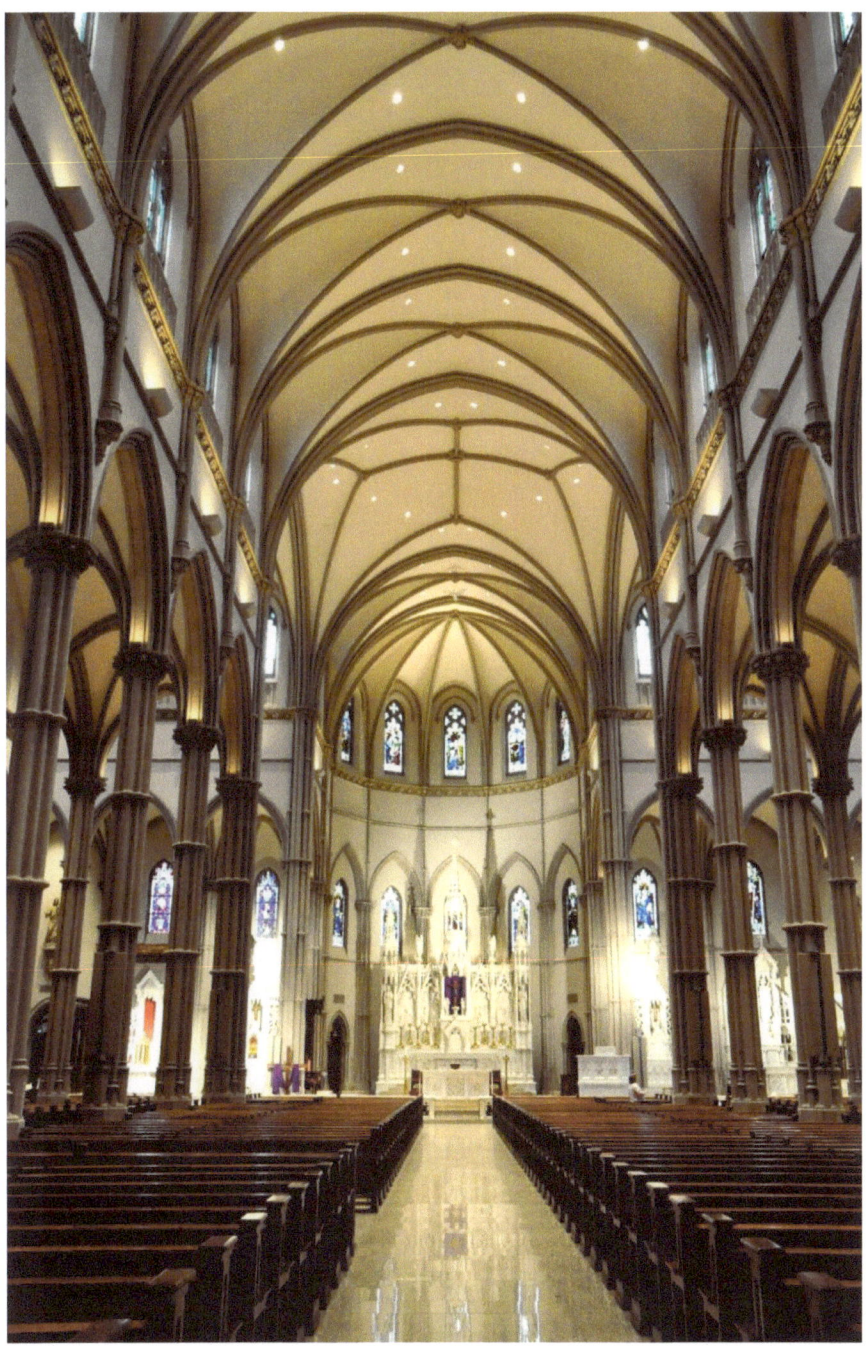

relocating to its current Oakland home. Also on the North Side, Art Rooney, future athlete, sports promoter, and Hall-of-Fame football patriarch, still wore knickers and lived above his father's saloon.

Except for Mr. Carnegie's Institute, Oakland was new ground, the new frontier, but Bishop Phelan was betting on it. Carefully measuring the decidedly low-rise neighborhood, he recreated it as his cathedral town, Pittsburgh's version of Coventry, or Chartres. Here, at least, the Cathedral's twin towers would dominate the landscape -- which they did, for some three decades, until that upstart Pitt Chancellor John Bowman's own secular Cathedral of Learning dwarfed everything else in the city.

Overseen in all its details by Bishop Regis Canevin after Bishop Phelan's untimely 1904 death, opening in 1906, St. Paul Cathedral cost some $1.1 million. Designed in 14th-century Flemish Gothic style, it seats 1,800, stands nearly 250 feet tall, and contains a wondrous blend of pointed arches, ribbed cross vaults, and oceans of stained glass. Following the medieval dictum that the church should teach and inspire, that congregants receive the Gospel from the building itself, and that moving through shadow and light be a spiritual journey, St. Paul Cathedral engages its congregants on their spiritual quest.

With more than 100 stained glass windows, the largest 37 feet by 22 feet, the smallest 27 by 16 inches, congregants are surrounded by some 45 saints, 25 biblical scenes, 30 scriptural verses, and the Great Seal of the United States, all fabricated locally by Willet Stained Glass, along with firms in Munich, Birmingham, New York, and Cleveland. Along the walls, Joseph Sibbel's one-of-a-kind cast-bronze Stations of the Cross are framed in African marble and topped with crosses carved from Holy Land olive wood. High on the walls, a frieze figures indigenous Pennsylvania fauna and flora -- ruffed grouse, grey squirrels, oak leaves, and grapes.

Bishop Phelan's monument, St. Paul Cathedral is Pittsburgh's third catholic cathedral, the Oakland church preceded by two structures at Fifth and Grant, across from the Chislett Courthouse (1841-82). In 1843 a church built nine years prior at a cost of $40,000 was converted into a cathedral when Pittsburgh was elevated to a diocese -- and the new bishop needed a seat. Standing for 18 years, the cathedral suspiciously burned down in 1851. (This was the height of the Know Nothing anti-Catholic era, and while arson was strongly suspected, it was never proved.)

Replaced by a grander structure in 1855, this is the building -- and the land -- which Bishop Phelan left in 1901. Designed in part by Charles Bartberger, Pittsburgh's first great post-1845 fire architect, the cathedral joined such Bartberger landmarks as the First Presbyterian Church (since replaced), Eberhardt-Ober Brewery (North Side), and St. Michael the Archangel Church (South Side). With the cornerstone laid just six weeks after the fire, the new church cost $170,000 and was consecrated in 1855.

Considered at the time as America's finest cathedral, this St. Paul featured an octagonal dome and Parisian papier-mâché Stations of the Cross.

When its replacement rose in a scant three years -- a time signature simply impossible to imagine today -- St. Paul opened with a Solemn Pontifical Mass of Consecration, honored dignitaries wearing top hats, streetside spectators decked out in black derbies.

St. Paul's first century has seen many noted moments, some solemn, some joyous. Walt Harper played jazz there, as did Mary Lou Williams. Sir Gilbert Levine conducted the Mendelssohn Choir.

On the sadder side of the ledger, funeral masses have marked the untimely passing of Mayors Richard Caliguiri, 1988, and Bob O'Connor, 2006. For labor leader Philip Murray's 1952 funeral, St. Paul was SRO, with more than 4,000 standing outside.

Yet aside from being a breathtaking historical structure, "the cathedral is very much alive," says Father Donald Breier, the church's pastor as well as the cathedral's rector. Alive, he adds, all the time, with neighborhood residents; students; and international visitors to Pitt, Carnegie Mellon, and UPMC. "People not of our faith come here, too," he adds, "not just to look at the architecture, but to enjoy an oasis of quiet in an area full of noise." As such, unlike many churches, the cathedral stays open all day so that people "can experience that quiet and find peace in their lives," Father Breier says.

Asking for everything from guidance to absolution, everyone from students to street people show up in Father Breier's confessional. Sometimes, he says, they just need someone kind and understanding -- and anonymous -- to hear them. For his part, Father Breier listens, counsels, advises, invariably directs the non-Catholics to their own faith communities. While the building may be one of Pittsburgh's premier cathedrals, "this," he smiles, "is a very interesting ministry."

CHAPTER TWENTY-THREE

EAST LIBERTY PRESBYTERIAN CHURCH

T hey demurred at first, over this, their magnificent fifth church, fearing that with a $4 million price tag (in Depression-era dollars) they would never be able to maintain the building. So the Mellon family upped the ante, adding an endowment for upkeep -- which today runs to $1 million per annum "just to keep the doors open," says the East Liberty Presbyterian Church's Pastor, the Reverend Doctor Randall K. Bush -- Randy to everyone. With the proverbial pot thus sweetened, the church elders accepted the gift, their soaring, neo-Gothic masterpiece in the heart of East Liberty.

The story begins a long time prior to that, when Pittsburgh was a series of farming villages. In 1778, as the Revolution still raged, Alexander Negley became the first permanent resident in what became East Liberty. (At the time, a liberty was land set aside for grazing cattle.) A staunch settler, he called the area Negleytown; a proper Presbyterian, he gathered about him like-minded co-religionists and set about going to church. They could sojourn west, to Pittsburgh, to the First Presbyterian Church, or east, to Beulah Presbyterian, amid the pastures and the fields. In between, however, were bad roads, especially with the autumn rains and winter snows, and bad guys, in the form of earlier inhabitants, who often took armed exception to their newer, paler neighbors.

Between muddy ruts and marauding natives, the group took to having Sunday meetings in the Negley homestead. By 1789, the group, having swelled to some 41 members, began their own church.

It took 20 years, but in 1809 Alexander's son Jacob built a 16-by-20 frame structure, on the site of the current church, as a religious school and meeting house. (That school stood until 1835, and in the era before public education, taught many of the congregation's children, including Sarah Negley, later Mrs. Sarah Negley Mellon, wife of Judge Thomas Mellon, progenitor of the family banking fortune.)

Within a decade, East Liberty had grown so quickly that in late 1818 the congregation needed a real church. Tapping nearly 100 subscribers -- the donor list reading like a *Who's Where of Pittsburgh Streets*: Negley, Herron, Peebles, McCaslin, Roup, Bingham, and Dahlem -- they raised $1,500.

The next year, 1819, the first church arose -- on an acre-and-a-half of land donated by the Negley family. With the 44-by-44 brick building boasting two stories, the church stood until 1862, becoming the East Liberty Academy after it was defrocked. Now the First Presbyterian Church of East Liberty, they greeted their first pastor, William B. McIlvane, in 1830. Although his starting salary was a bargain-basement $500, something must have endeared the congregation to him, and vice versa, because he held the post for the next 40 years.

Growth continuing, by 1847 they needed another building. Opening in 1848, the 50-by-70 red brick church featured a $90 interior fresco.

Things might have continued that way -- slow but steady growth as East Liberty matured from a farming into a mercantile community -- but for two external factors. The first, in 1852, was the arrival of the Pennsylvania Railroad, which brought unprecedented commerce to the area; the second, in 1861, was the American Civil War, which recreated Pittsburgh into the Arsenal of the Republic.

Overnight, East Liberty -- literally rolling in wealth and teeming with new people -- needed a larger church, built in 1864, signature steeple on the left.

Peace brought gas lighting into the church, which rebranded itself as the East Liberty Presbyterian Church. Improvements continued, not the least of which was Mrs. Negley's 1867 gift of a 2,760-pound bell. "Doubtless," Georgina Negley wrote in her celebratory *Centennial* accounting, "other bells have rung from this place of worship in the early days, but for more than fifty years this bell, so familiar to us, has pealed in melodious tones the Gospel message, 'Come.'" (Aside from calling the faithful to prayer, the bell tolled for solemn civic occasions as well, including President McKinley's funeral train and the November 1918 Armistice.)

By the mid '80s it was clear they had to build again. Opening in 1888, the all-electric fourth church was buttressed by donations by such families as Mellon, Negley, Heinz, Bigelow, King, Aiken, and Fisher.

Perhaps that great stone church might still be standing save for Richard Beatty Mellon and Jennie King Mellon, whose idea it was to create a fitting memorial to their mothers, Sarah Jane Negley Mellon and Sarah Cordelia Smith King.

"The general style is Gothic, of course," wrote famed architect Ralph Adams Cram, the church's designer, "for this was the supreme expression of Christian civilization brought into being to express in the fullest degree the ethos and the operation of the Christian

religion." Picking up what he called "suggestions" from England, France, and Spain, Cram created the plans, and in 1931 Mellon himself laid the cornerstone.

Dying in 1933, Mellon could not attend the twice-weekly planning meetings held at the Duquesne Club. Nor did he see his creation take life. Opening, fittingly enough, on Mother's Day, 1935, East Liberty Presbyterian drew some 5,500 people -- 1,700 seated, the rest listening throughout the church. Standing some 300 feet high, it is so grand and breath-taking a structure that neighborhood children were convinced that the quartz specs sparkling in the surrounding sidewalks were really diamonds.

What the Mellons got for their money was 220,000 square feet of building, including the main sanctuary, chapel (now the home of the Taizé new-age ecumenical services), enclosed courtyard, administrative offices, music rehearsal suite, basketball court, and four-lane duck-pin bowling alley.

The main sanctuary alone is worth the price of admission. With the stained glass windows designed by Charles Connick, the themes are secular, American, and Presbyterian. Aside from many standard biblical characters and scenes, featured prominently are famed poets Longfellow, Burns, Tennyson, and Whittier. The Pilgrims at Cape Cod stand *here*, the reformed church in New Amsterdam rests *there*. Franklin and Lincoln come from American history, as does the figure in the church's most notorious window, the famous slave owner, traitor to the Republic, and staunch Presbyterian, Confederate General Thomas "Stonewall" Jackson.

Major Presbyterian countries are represented by their national flowers carved throughout the church, the Dutch tulip, French lily, Scotch thistle, English rose, and Irish shamrock.

They even designed their own coat of arms -- a cross, Bible, and the checked Pittsburgh tartan.

"Of all the cathedrals and churches I have built," Ralph Adams Cram summed up, "this is my masterpiece. This church has been the most profound spiritual experience of my life."

With the congregation largely white, and wealthy, through the early 1960s ushers wore morning suits. But no Pittsburgh neighborhood was bruised as badly by urban renewal as East Liberty, and the once-stately environs suffered a spectacular decline. Rebranding itself once more, as The Cathedral of Hope, the racially diverse congregation has a decided outward focus, sponsoring Hope Academy, the Good Samaritan Soup Kitchen, homeless shelter, food pantry, and so on.

There is room for this, and more, in a magnificently designed, lovingly kept building. Pastor Randy Bush gestures around him. "It's an amazing place," he says.

CHAPTER TWENTY-FOUR

HEINZ MEMORIAL CHAPEL

In some ways, this is a tale of money and power and will. A true Pittsburgh story – how great things get done, often because of one person's vision, and another person's ability to pay for it.
There have been countless times in countless houses of worship when a single charismatic leader convinces others to give – and design beyond what they had previously thought possible.
Such was Heinz Chapel.
It begins with the legendary University of Pittsburgh Chancellor John Bowman, creator of the landmark Cathedral of Learning, perhaps the greatest fund-raiser in the city's history.
Starting as a vague gift -- H.J. Heinz himself, who died in 1919, wanted to honor his mother, Anna Margaretta Heinz, with what he had called "a building" at the University.
With heavy negotiations following, by the 1930s Chancellor Bowman had ratcheted up the "building" to a million-dollar non-denominational memorial chapel celebrating three millenia of religious and secular achievement. As he presciently put it when they laid the cornerstone, "the chapel is designed as a fitting center of worship which in various ways will rise at the University. The character, intensity, the level of that worship may change from generation to generation. The spiritual tide in men rises and falls. Through these changes, though, the Chapel will stand, calm and undisturbed."
While that certainly was his fervent wish, and while the Chapel has indeed stood as a place of blessed respite for more than 70 years, like many other houses of worship its conception and gestation were not so peaceful.
From all accounts, while Mr. Bowman may have led the band, Mr. Howard Heinz was *in charge*. With ground was broken in 1933, the cornerstone laid in 1934, Heinz spent the succeeding four years -- until the chapel was dedicated in 1938 -- supervising every detail in the building (as H.J. Heinz II did with the Penn Theatre's transformation into Heinz Hall some three decades later.)
First, the building's design. Sending his personal representative to Europe to tour cathedrals, Heinz settled *not* on a direct copy of anything, as many erroneously believe, but instead, working with Charles Klauder of Philadelphia, on a 253-foot tall neo-gothic church with hints of Rouen, Chartres, hither, and yon. "That process," says Chapel Director Patricia Gibbons, "was just incredible."
Next, the artistry. Although the hand-carved stone and woodwork are extraordinary, the soaring, 73-feet-high stained-glass windows are the Chapel's *sine qua non*.

Choosing Amerca's premier stained-glass fabricator -- Pittsburgher Charles Connick, who had relocated to Boston -- Heinz stood his ground about everything from color to installation. In one instance, with half a transept window set, Heinz, unhappy with the color, had it removed, shipped back to Boston, and completely re-done. "He exercised great care and attention to detail," Gibbons says.

When the stained glass cooled, Connick surveyed his 23 windows, covering 4,000 square feet, containing nearly a quarter-million pieces of glass, and depicting 391 identifiable people, and considered it the finest work he had ever done. (Astonishingly, this was only one of 316 commissions in 19 states on which Connick worked from the time he signed the Heinz Chapel contract until he finished.)

Winding up with an entire course in Western Civ, there are renderings of a whole host of people -- for openers, King David shares space with St. Francis of Assisi, Leonardo da Vinci, Sir Isaac Newton, Louis Pasteur, William Wordsworth, Abraham Lincoln, and Ralph Waldo Emerson. Women's Christian Temperance Union doyenne Frances Willard even makes an appearance, lecturing President Grover Cleveland about the evils of Demon Rum.

Then there's the Boone family -- Dan'l & Co., Lewis & Clark, Christopher Columbus, Moses, Jesus, Florence Nightingale, Emily Dickinson (the famously reclusive poet who'd be surprised at being remembered – much less depicted), Clara Barton (at the Johnstown Flood), Emily Bronte (the world's most famous one-book wonder), Johnny Appleseed, and so many, many more.

Although the windows were fabricated entirely in Boston, all the altar wood (which, legend has it, all came from a single Sherwood Forest oak tree) was carved on site. Indeed, it was a busy site -- between carvers and installers, there could be as many as 90 artisans at once in nascent Heinz Chapel – including, for example, a man to test the windows' waterproofing. (The records remember him only as Jimmy.)

While in the Great Depression the highest-paid artisans received the princely sum of 25 cents an hour, now, of course, the windows alone are priceless -- and entirely irreplaceable. For its part, the Connick studio closed in 1989. What's more, Gibbons says, "even if you had the money, you couldn't find the craftsmen."

All told, from drawings to dedication, including all the glass, all the hard-carved stone and woodwork, even the 800-pound doors, Heinz Memorial Chapel cost the then-princely sum of $1 million -- astounding in the Great Depression, literally incalculable today.

An irony: the Chapel's only change since its opening was a 1995 handicapped access. In these inflationary times, a mere 60 years after its construction, Heinz Chapel's new side entrance, elevator, and wheelchair ramp – all standard stuff -- cost exactly the same.

Far from being a museum, or a relic from a more pious era, Heinz Chapel hosts some 1,500 events every year. Roughly 100,000 people come for religious services, concerts (often on the magnificent 4,272-pipe Reuter Organ, the Chapel's third), classes, memorial services, and tours. Open for weddings, anyone can rent the hall, and do, some 180 times every year. Some people actually like getting married in Heinz Chapel so much they return multiple times for multiple marriages.

As with any house of worship, some are drawn less by the Chapel's splendor than by its air of hushed reverence, its quiet sanctuary.

While most Heinz Chapel events are relatively intimate affairs, the largest in memory was the 1991 funeral for Senator John Heinz. Attracting the entire Senate and Vice President Quayle, "it was totally unprecedented," Gibbons recalls. "It is the ultimate event we will ever do here" -- especially, she adds, since Heinz Chapel never hosts funerals. Memorial services, certainly, for university-related people, but never funerals. "It is a *school* chapel," she emphasizes, and Heinz family tradition dictates that there be no funerals (except for family members, of course.)

The Secret Service came for that one, as they did -- complete with sharpshooters stationed on the roof -- for an appearance by Vice President Al Gore.

By contrast, the largest non-event in Heinz Chapel history was Philippe Petit's proposed high-wire walk from the Chapel spire to the Cathedral of Learning. Although the French aerialist had impeccable credentials -- including the daring 1974 walk between New York City's Twin Towers, and similar jaunts between Paris' Notre Dame Cathedral Towers and Australia's Sydney Harbour Bridge Towers -- ultimately the University nixed it.

Then there are other, quieter moments, no photographers, no press. Like the Marine Lt. Colonel who came alone to remember his fellow soldiers who had been killed in Iraq. "Did it give him some sort of peace?" Patricia Gibbons asks. "I hope so." She pauses. "That's the kind of thing that makes opening our doors worthwhile."

CHAPTER TWENTY-FIVE

HINDU JAIN TEMPLE

It's 1:30 in the afternoon. A small, dapper, barefooted man, dressed in a white shirt and tan slacks strides purposefully across the carpeted floor, rings a bell, then prostrates himself before a pair of Hindu deities, incarnations of Vishnu, sustainer of the universe, and Lakshmi, his wife, goddess of prosperity. The man's brief ablutions finished, he rises, turns, and leaves, as crisply, and silently, as he entered.

"Shoes," explains Sashi Prabhu, the Hindu Jain Temple secretary, "go everywhere.

When you come inside the Temple, you don't want to bring in unclean material. It's also a matter of respect -- you don't want to make yourself taller or bigger. If you're full of ego, you cannot approach God."

The bell, very much like that found on a ship, "lets the Almighty know you're here," she gestures. "It also helps you dispel any negative thoughts. Prostration," Prabhu adds, "demonstrates respect. If we worship Vishnu with love and devotion, then Lakshmi will enrich our lives."

It all takes place in a large, white room containing many deities in many niches, large and small, all the subject of individual devotions. "When you have a certain feeling you

go to that god," Prabhu says. "All forms of Vishnu come to the Earth for different purposes. Whenever there is unrighteousness on the earth, the Lord takes a form to get things right."

"Some friends are favorites," adds Vinod Pandey, one of three Hindu priests stationed at the Hindu Jain Temple. "Best friends."

There are hand-carved white lions as well, "to keep the demons away," Prabhu says. Many deities are dressed in red and yellow, she adds, because they are "auspicious colors." "Yellow," Pandey says, "increases spirituality, while red is very, very blessed. White is knowledge. Green is prosperity -- and internal happiness."

"Art is a very big part of our religion," Prabhu says. "We believe that all forms of art are God-given gifts. Here, people express their talents. It's very creative."

"Here at the Temple," she adds, "there's always something going on. We're open seven days a week. There are daily services morning and evening. All three priests are always busy." She pauses to smile. "There's no appointment necessary. Everyone is welcome."

As it should be. Perhaps Western Pennsylvania's most imaginative use of red brick, it would seem that the spectacular Hindu Jain Temple landed here directly from Northern India. With the domes, topped with 24-karat gold foil, representing "different deities and powers," says Shubha Mullick, the Temple president, the elephants guarding the entrance "symbolize good luck," she adds.

It took a bit of that luck, and a lot of hard work, to build it. Beginning as an idea some 40 years ago, when the then-small Pittsburgh-based Indian community began meeting in a Squirrel Hill basement, they sought a way to create a worship space -- or worship spaces -- for their growing communities, the Southern and Northern Hindus, Sikhs, and Jains. Although they all have different religious observances -- markedly so -- they banded together, forming the Pittsburgh chapter of the Hindu Temple Society of North America.

In April, 1973, when a suburban Baptist Church said it could no longer afford its modest building and surrounding seven acres, the tiny Temple Society tightened its belt and, at an assessment of $200 a family, raised the $10,000 down payment -- then an enormous sum for young emigrées with growing families.

Beginning simply, in the former one-story church, they had none of the standard accoutrements -- no prayer niches, no marble or stone deities, no clergy. Instead, they settled for a low stage filled with framed images of a wide variety of divine manifestations, each group conducting its own service, the collective meeting Sunday afternoons over vegetarian pot-luck lunches to discuss plans for a new building that would more properly house them all.

These being religious people, of course there were the inevitable schisms, the Southern Hindus building the Sri Venkateswara Temple on the Parkway East, the Sikhs moving into their own Gurdwara. Because the remaining Northern Hindus and Jains were barely able to raise the $300 monthly fee for mortgage and upkeep, there were real fears that the hoped-for Unity Temple would die stillborn.

Refusing to give up, they continued planning, this time for an $800,000 building -- which they simply could not afford. Setting the bar a bit lower, they designed a preliminary $125,000 structure, with no extraordinary exterior sculpture, which would house five deities. Miraculously, donors came forth, including those who mortgaged their homes to raise the necessary funds. Pledging the money in late 1980, they broke ground the following year.

At first, a basic shell for the Temple was created by local artisans, and with an Indian philanthropist helping out, they pushed on ahead, eventually constructing a building in

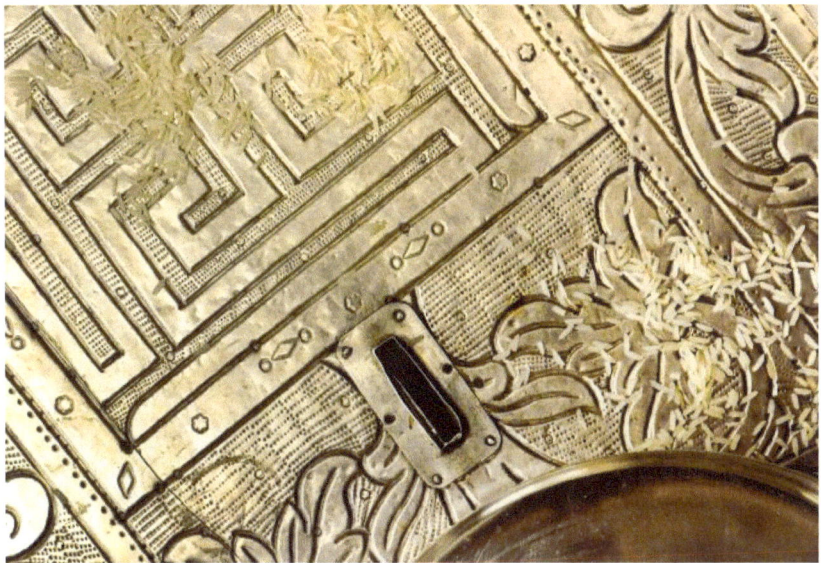

the style of a third-century Nagradi Temple. In May 1984, they celebrated Pran Pratishtha, the ceremony which infuses Divine Breath into the murtis, transforming them from statues into deities. When 2,000 people came, from Pittsburgh, surrounding states, some from India itself, the Hindu Jain Temple had finally arrived.

Still, work continued. In 1987, an architect from India was called upon to design the elegant exterior. With Indian artisans coming in 1988 to create the extensive, elaborate carvings, all construction was finally completed in September 1990.

Operating today with some 600 families -- 75 percent Hindus, 25 percent Jains -- it stands as the first unified Hindu Jain Temple in North America, perhaps in the world, and is a unique example of the group's understanding, tolerance, and appreciation of other religious practices. "We are very flexible," Prabhu says.

Such flexibility is vital when two religions share the same space. While both the Hindus and the Jains value such core beliefs as truth, tolerance, and peace, the Jains, who are accorded their own worship space in the Temple, follow a path of non-violence towards all living things. Strict vegetarians, Jains will not eat root vegetables because the plant needs to be killed in order to be harvested. Often praying with their mouths covered, so as not to destroy anything that might happen by, Jains have their own deity, Parshwa Nathji Mahavir Swami, the statue representing a person who lived some 2,500 years ago and attained a state of perfect enlightenment through meditation.

"People say that Hindus are idol worshippers," Swami Chidanand Saraswatiji, the Hindu Jain Temple's spiritual head, has written. "We are not. We are ideal worshippers. It is not the plaster and marble and stone we revere; rather, it is the presence of God which has been transmitted into these otherwise lifeless statues...God is kind and merciful enough to infuse our deities with His Divine Presence and allow Himself to be worshipped through these deities. The deities in the Temple serve as a window to the Divine. Through fixing our eyes upon the image, we are able to catch a glimpse of the Supreme Reality."

CHAPTER TWENTY-SIX

THE PRESBYTERIAN CHURCH OF SEWICKLEY

"What continent am I on?", a visitor to The Presbyterian Church of Sewickley (TPCS to the cognescenti) cried out not so long ago, and with good reason. Escorted into the entry hall, he stood amongst Tudor trappings, including a large tapestry out of Edmund Spenser's *The Faerie Queene*, Book I, Red Crosse slaying the Dragon before Gloriana herself.

Well, we know where *these* roots are.

The 19th Century had barely turned when a core group of dedicated Presbyterians began holding religious services in the so-called Sewickley Bottoms. Meeting in homes, barns, and, weather permitting, under the oak trees along Hoey's Run, the group of Scotch-Irish devotees shortly joined with co-religionists who had staked their claims along Big Sewickley Creek.

Enjoying the ministrations of itinerant pastors, in 1808 the group petitioned the Presbytery in nearby Pittsburgh to send clergy on a more regular basis. Four years later, in 1812, the new congregation had grown to 20 members, enough for them to create a formal church.

A frontier-style building followed six years later, in 1818, made of logs and clapboard. Sewickley farming was good, and river trade was better, and within a dozen years the Presbyterians needed both a full-time pastor and a larger worship space. With the arrival of Daniel Nevin, then a recent graduate of Pittsburgh's Western Theological Seminary, the Sewickley congregation requested that the Pittsburgh Presbytery formally recognize it. To this day, February 17, 1838, is celebrated as Founders' Day. (A century later, Bayard Christy characterized those early settlers as "farmers and artisans and shopkeepers. They were humble people; they lived from hand to mouth.")

Two years later, in 1840, Sewickley's Presbyterian Church moved into a new brick structure. By 1843, membership rolls hovered at 60, where it seemed they might remain forever.

Then the railroad changed The Presbyterian Church of Sewickley forever.

Previously, Sewickley was a horse-and-buggy town -- a sleepy riverside village, if you prefer. Suddenly, the population exploded. The Pittsburgh, Fort Wayne, and Chicago hauled in residents -- and industry. Overnight, church membership jumped to 235, requiring a new, larger building -- their third. Now officially called the Presbyterian Church of Sewickleyville, and led by the Shields, Nevin, Oliver, and Champ families, in 1859 the congregation paid $1,250 for TPCS' signature site, Grant and Beaver Streets.

Two years later, the church with the two-feet-thick stone walls was completed at a cost of $12,500. (Over the years, there've been three significant additions, in 1913, 1951-53, and 1996, all retaining the flavor of the original.)

For their Golden Anniversary, in 1888, the Reverend James Allison summed up Presbyterian life at the Sewickley church by saying that "here many of its inmates first felt the word of God come with power to their hearts; here many of those now widely dispersed – not a few of whom have already ascended on high – were born into the kingdom of God."

Then he turned his attention to what he -- and many others -- called The War for the Suppression of the Rebellion: "The first gun fired on Sumter aroused the patriotism of this entire community, as much as that of any other part of the land. The people of this church had laid their children on God's altar, and now they willingly, along with other denominations, devoted them to the service of their country. Within the walls of the present house of worship, before the pews were put in place, our noble young men met for drill from night to night. And when they left for the field, we followed them with our tears and our prayers; and alas! many of them never returned to us."

By the Gay '90s, Pittsburgh was enjoying previously unimagined riches, none of which bypassed Sewickley. Replacing the church's clear glass windows, they sought the grandest stained glass artists of the day, including John LaFarge, Louis Comfort Tiffany, Pittsburgh native Charles Connick, and Howard Wilbert. The result was perhaps the region's finest collection of disparate ecclesiastical stained glass.

Nevertheless, the splendid environs could not keep world events from the Presbyterian Church's doors. During World War I, doughboys bivouacked there -- as had the Grand Army of the Republic during the Civil War. All the while, the good Presbyterian women used their foot-pedaled machines to sew mittens, sweaters, and hats, handing them out to the troops as trains crept through Sewickley station.

Hardly was the war over when the Influenza Epidemic struck, and the church was transformed into a hospital to house some of the thousands afflicted in greater Pittsburgh.

War came again, and again the Presbyterian Church answered the call. In the 1940s, donating their ration stamps and food grown in their own Victory gardens, the members operated a cafeteria often serving 100 dinners a night to the shipbuilders working on nearby Neville Island.

Time, tide, and Pittsburgh winters being what they are, they've had to touch up the old girl over the years. For example, the century-old wooden roof was removed in the '70s, reinforced with steel trusses, and replaced. "It looks deceptively simple up there," architect David Shaw shakes his head, "but it isn't."

In the main church the priceless Tiffany, Connick, et. al. windows were cleaned and re-leaded at a cost of $50,000 each. While they were at it, they replaced the old carpet, which was so thick that "when you sang," Shaw recalls, "you couldn't hear your own voice." Now, the sound moves nicely around the grand space.

A new organ – so central to their services – came at a price of $700,000. That's the new price: the old price was that when the first one was installed the church suffered a schism over whether they should have one of the newfangled things at all. The modernists ultimately won that argument, as they did over the change from long Scottish-style sermons to more hymns and more contemporary music. "The culture of the Presbyterian Church is much more inclusive than it was before," Shaw says.

Home to some 1,500 people – these days referred to as 600 giving units – they include scions of some of Pittsburgh's foremost folks, including descendents of the Way, Oliver, Shields, Magee, Frick, Semple, Arrott, Nevin, and McKnight families, among others.

One frequent visitor, Fred Rogers, came and sat in the back, concerned that his celebrity would overshadow the services. Another is Mario Lemieux, who drops his kids off at day care.

Like many contemporary churches, the Presbyterian Church is a haven for such support groups as Alcoholics Anonymous, Overeaters Anonymous, Narcotics Anonymous, and, on a less life-threatening basis, the Boy Scouts. "We open the building to a lot of public uses," Shaw says, including refugees from Bhutan, Habitat for Humanity efforts, even relief teams sent after Katrina.

Still, for all the changes, for all the glory and the grandeur, at its heart, in the quiet, wooded anterooms, and the small, French-style Chapel of the Resurrection, the church exudes an ineffable feeling of sanctuary, of solitude and reflection. Perhaps, after two centuries, that's what brings people back.

"I have been young and am young no longer," Bayard Christy wrote in 1938. "This always has been my church."

CHAPTER TWENTY-SEVEN

CALVARY UNITED METHODIST CHURCH

The workmen are crawling all over Calvary United Methodist Church like ants, the office furniture is piled in *that* corner, and the Reverend Larry Homitksy – wearing his holiday finest T-shirt and stained jeans – is in a complete tizzy. After all, the storm busted through his architectural gem of a church on the North Side, and they've got to fix it up *pronto*! before the paint starts to peel and the wood rots.

Dating back more than 200 years, when the first area Methodists founded a meeting house Downtown, this version came about through fire and schism. Having built a fine church at Smithfield and Forbes, future site of Mr. Kaufmann's Clock, in 1890 they watched it burn. Homeless, the congregation split, half going to Shadyside to found the First United Methodist Church, half moving out to the 'burbs, near Millionaires Row in the City of Allegheny.

Money they had, and the handiwork they commissioned is not merely priceless today – it is simply unimaginable. To begin with, the doyens sent an architect to tour Europe for a year, copying here, cribbing there, creating a kind of French-style mini-cathedral. (Howard Heinz would do the same for his family's Pitt campus chapel some 40 years later.)

On Christmas Eve 1893, they opened their small, round church, what they later called the Chapel. Two years later, Spring 1895, the main Church was dedicated -- neo-French Gothic with hand-carved gargoyles, two mismatched spires (reminiscent of Chartres), St. Andrew's Crosses, angels in the Cleveland bluestone, a vaulted oak ceiling, and some of the world's greatest -- and now entirely irreplaceable -- Tiffany windows. (A century later, it cost some $300,000 simply to clean and re-lead them.)

Among the five dozen ministers present that grand day in 1895 were Bishop Matthew Simpson of the Methodist Episcopal Church, and Dr. E. H. Gray, the Baptist chaplain of the Senate and pastor of the E. Street Baptist church. Bishop Simpson, who subsequently performed the marriage of Robert Todd Lincoln, gave the opening prayer and Dr. Gray gave the closing prayer.

Surely these august churchmen knew that in their day, the 1890s, the average church cost something between $13,000 and $23,000. By contrast, Calvary United Methodist cost an eye-popping $220,000. How many millions would that be today – if you could find the stone masons, carpenters, woodworkers, and of course glassmakers to recreate it?

In his largest-ever commission, Lewis Comfort Tiffany fashioned windows for Mr. Joseph Horne and his brother-in-law and partner, Mr. Christian Bernard Shea. Windows so stunning that, at the right time of day, when the light flows in at Beech and Allegheny, they broadcast rainbows all over the walls. Another age would have called it psychedelic. Now, we'll simply say it's breath-taking.

Fashioned of thick, layered glass, a cornucopia of rich color, and figured in incredible detail, one memorable panel portrays a highly corporeal Christ walking bodily from the tomb. Certainly, there are heavenly depictions as well, but this, the most earthly, symbolizes their Methodist ministry, the here and now, the insistence that personal salvation occurs with service to the world.

Despite a century of use, and an extreme makeover, much of the original church survives, including the green pew pads manufactured by Mr. Joseph Horne's company, the oak pews themselves, and the old oaken ceiling – the reversed hull of a ship, symbolic of the vehicle that God provides in the midst of need, in the time of trouble. And for the founders, those troubles seemed very far away indeed.

"For a long time," Larry Homitsky says, "it was the church where the rich people went."

But cities evolve and neighborhoods change. Roughly 80 years after its grand opening, the church – like so many before and after it -- was ready to close.

It was something of a miracle that Calvary United Methodist didn't. Hanging on through the grit and stubbornness of a congregation that refused to see the building torn down -- or turned into a hookah bar -- it limped into its second century. With the dust and decay of 100 years washed off due in no small measure to $1.3 million raised by the Allegheny Historical Preservation Society, and some two dozen foundations that helped, the church stands stalwart on the North Side.

But that's not what Larry Homitsky wants to talk about, all this artwork, and ancient history, and antiquarians who don't live here anymore. "How do you create a ministry?" he asks. "Not just a museum. A *presence*."

Simply, you get out and minister.

Leaving the suburbs, the gentle, good-natured father of five came to Calvary United Methodist in August 2008. And he came with hope.

"One of the direct correlatives to that hope is leadership," he says. "For too long, we shifted the brightest and the best to the suburbs. Now, there's tremendous hope for urban settings. There's hope when leadership gives resources and talent to those areas.

"I see hope in the faces here," he adds. "They want to make a difference in the world."

Did they do this in the early days, run a soup kitchen when the Hornes and Sheas and their friends from nearby Millionaires Row worshipped here? While that answer is lost to history, they sure do now, feeding upwards of 125 homeless people three times every week, Tuesday, Thursday, and Sunday (except for Steelers home Sundays, when the

pickin's are better at the tailgate parties.) Operating three active Homeless Ministry sites, including Arch Street and North Avenue, Calvary United Methodist also hosts such vital scion societies as Gamblers Anonymous, Alcoholics Anonymous, and Narcotics Anonymous.

During the school year, they sponsor a children's choir; in the summer there's Vacation Bible School – in that garden getaway spot, Northview Heights – which draws upwards of five dozen children.

"We have young families coming back," Homitsky says proudly, "multi-racial and all economic levels." Granted, some may come merely to have their weddings in a spectacular setting – but they find themselves returning for worship and service. "The reason this site has more hope and potential is its history," he allows. "It is an inspiring site. But its history is a tie to the future. They come for the windows -- and stay for the programs."

Such as Mission in Vision – in which 300 people, half of them homeless, got free eye exams and free eye glasses. So important are these glasses, Homitsky adds, that he's no longer surprised to see a man jump out of bushes and proudly brandish his new specs. "Hey, Reverend," he'll shout, "I still got 'em."

Then there was the time they coordinated with a Manchester elementary school reading program, taking three dozen kids to an eye clinic, getting many new glasses. "That," Larry Homitsky smiles in his good Methodist way, "was an exciting day.

"It's making a difference where you're at," he adds, then pauses. "That may not be everything, but it's a start."

CHAPTER TWENTY-EIGHT

St. Benedict the Moor Church

He stands like a sentinel above the Hill District, arms stretched wide in welcome, reveling in his commanding view of Downtown and the Allegheny River. High above Crawford Street, high above Freedom Corner, he greets all comers, black and white, rich and poor, parishioners as well as refugees from the wide world beyond.

He is Saint Benedict the Moor, a 16th-century Franciscan, an illiterate slaves' son, cook and counselor, a gentle man with such extraordinary curative powers that in 1807 he was canonized, named patron saint of African-Americans.

While he may seem like nothing so much as a nice piece of statuary, his front-row perch created in 1968 by the noted artist Frederick Shrady, at St. Benedict the Moor Church they take the man and his mission literally. To wit, celebrating their heritage while welcoming all, creating a haven for the tempest-tossed.

Midwifed in 1889 by the first National Congress of Black Catholics, convened in Washington to demand greater visibility for African-Americans in the church, the fathers at Holy Ghost College (now Duquesne University) on the next hilltop established St. Benedict the Moor as the first African-American parish in the Pittsburgh Diocese. With the current church an amalgam of four black churches (including Saint Brigid, Saint Richard, and Holy Trinity), the congregation has been housed in its signature space since 1893.

Over the decades, the very building has grown to stand as a symbol of Black pride in the Hill District -- as well as a line of demarcation against the rapacious redevelopment of the Lower Hill, where a thriving neighborhood simply disappeared beneath the bulldozers' blades, and some 8,000 people were dispossessed, scattered in the street to find replacement housing on their own.

As it happens, the church's founders could not have chosen a more imposing piece of stage setting -- and while not part of St. Benedict the Moor *per se*, its location has indelibly linked it with events around it. For example, after the 1950s reconstruction of the Lower Hill, which ended at Crawford Street, plans were drawn for the 'dozers to roll east, further into the Hill. Rallying on the steps of St. Benedict the Moor, protestors proclaimed "Not another inch!" and erected an adjacent billboard with the message "No development beyond this point!" Facing death threats, the protestors marched to the City-County Building, eventually succeeding in stopping additional neighborhood demolition.

Dubbed Freedom Corner, the area became the focus for marches and demonstrations of all stripe, including acting as the debarkation point for more than 2,000 Pittsburghers who attended the 1963 March on Washington -- there to hear Dr. Martin Luther King's justly famous "I Have a Dream" speech.

Inside the 120-year-old church, with walls so white they nearly glow, and restrained stained glass windows figured in yellow, blue, and red, the sanctuary has enjoyed a moderate makeover, now redolent in African reds, greens, and blacks.

The saints came marching in, too, Saint Josephine Bakhita, a Sudanese slave; Saint Martin de Porres, a Peruvian mulatto; Saint Benedict; and Saint Charles Lwanga, a Ugandan martyr. One prominent wooden sculpture displays a decidedly African-looking Jesus welcoming the little children -- as St. Benedict the Moor welcomes its parishioners. For St. Benedict's whole is far greater than the sum of its many parts, its spirit far more than merely bricks and mortar, statuary and stained glass.

"I was looking for a family connection," comments Priscilla Davis. Now the parish secretary, she found her way to St. Benedict in 1992. "I started crying," she recalls. "I felt I was home."

Although drawing predominantly people of color, St. Benedict is a true rainbow coalition, attracting people of some 30 nationalities and ethnic groups -- as figured in representational flags hung all about the church proper -- as well as neighborhoods from all over the city, as seen in pins in a city map prominently displayed in the church lobby. *Auslanders* also include native Africans, Afro-Caribbeans, Native Americans, Mexicans, and Puerto Ricans. "We're a mixture of everything," says Alice Hartshorn, herself a member of the Kiowa tribe. "That was my draw to come here."

Like the congregation, the music's a bit of everything, too -- drums (bongos, tambourines, traps), keyboards (upright, electric, an antique organ so fine it draws musicians from all over the city). "Music plays a big part in worship and praise," Hartshorn says.

"It's always a celebration," says Joan Moran, who began commuting to St. Benedict from Donegal. "Children are also part of the congregation. They're a part of the noise."

All that noise packed into the standard 45-minute mass? Never! It's more like two hours, with the various musical selections, homilies, and peace (aka hugging all about the place.) "It never crossed our minds not to give hugs," Davis says. "We do so much together. Like families."

"Here we celebrate our humanity," Hartshorn adds. "Race, age, gender blend away as we enjoy the worship service."

They may come for the vibe -- gospel to gossip, confession to congas -- but for many the value added is AJAPO, for Acculturation for Justice, Access and Peace Outreach. Drawing refugees from the Sudan, Nigeria, Somalia, as well as the Caribbean -- the tortured, troubled spots of the earth -- "we are open to everybody," Moran says. "We minister to everyone in need." Thrown into the mix in 2001, Yinka Aganga-Williams -- Mama Yinka to scores of needy emigrées -- coordinates all AJAPO efforts. A Nigerian herself, whose connection to Pittsburgh began with children at nearby Duquesne University, she has seen her efforts to resettle -- and educate and assimilate -- 40 Sudanese refugees blossom into helping some 400 people every year. Needing everything -- from social services to children's services, good health to better language  -- "these are populations that have suffered a great deal," she gestures. "Some have been in refugee camps for five years. Some for 35 years." Aganga-Williams pauses. "They have known extreme hardship.

"For our part, we're able to see as a church that we have a responsibility to the public, to society. It's one thing for the church to give them spiritual food," she adds. "But this particular parish promotes the greater evangelization of God's church, to help these people's daily welfare and growth."

Like peeling back the layers of an onion to reveal a greater truth within, Aganga-Williams says there's a greater purpose at St. Benedict the Moor. "As these people grow," she says, "they're able to help the people back home." Social, spiritual, economic help -- it's all the same, and it's all in a direct line from the physical, pastoral, and spiritual care that Saint Benedict himself gave more than 400 years ago. And it doesn't stop at the church door. Or at the county line.

"It's not about social service for the purpose of social service," she shakes her head. "It's about bringing peace to the world."

CHAPTER TWENTY-NINE
St. Stanislaus Kostka Church

On a steamy Thursday morning while fans reluctantly move the sluggish, humid air around the 120-year-old church, volunteers scurry about, scrubbing and sweeping and hand-cleaning the place. They are loyal and loving – and few and far between.

"I was baptized here," one middle-aged woman says, rag in hand, bucket of soapy water at her feet, "and married here. My family's been coming here for 126 years, since before this building went up. My son is the 5th generation to be here. This morning," she gestures, "we've been working ourselves silly."

She's hardly the only one. Old buildings require constant vigilance, constant upkeep. St. Stanislaus Kostka -- St. Stan's, as everyone calls it -- at 21st and Smallman in the Strip is hardly an exception. The century-old pews -- which survived the 1936 St. Patrick's Day Flood, which covered them in mud, water, and silt -- need work, as does the floor, bearing the water scars like the scourges of non-believers. As do the water-pocked walls and chipped stained glass windows. In some ways, it's a miracle that any of them are left: after the December, 1936, explosion at the nearby Pittsburgh Banana Company, three of the medallion windows over the altars were so damaged that they were permanently covered.

But St. Stan's is a tough old bird, a survivor like the people who created it, and time and tide haven't been allowed to stop it. They were tough, the Poles who built Pittsburgh's first Polish church, tough and hard-working, in the mills, mines, and railroads; on the rivers and nearby produce yards. And they loved -- revered -- the story of St. Stanislaus Kostka, their patron. For his story is theirs, a story of epic journeys, of fierce struggles, ultimately of faith.

Born Stanislaus Kostka in 1550, at age 14 he was sent to a Vienna Jesuit school. Two years later, and severely ill, legend has it that angels brought him

the Blessed Sacrament -- and the Blessed Mother herself told him he was to enter the Society of Jesus. Because his father frowned on this activity, Stanislaus was turned away by the Vienna branch. Determined to fulfill his destiny, Stanislaus walked some 450 miles to Bavaria, where Peter Canisius welcomed the boy, then shipped him off to Rome. A scant nine months after joining the Jesuits, Stanislaus again took ill, dying at age 17 on the Feast of the Assumption, August 15th, 1568. He was canonized in 1726.

Perhaps it was his piety and early death, perhaps it was his epic journey -- like the one these parishioners made to America -- perhaps it was the danger in their lives, but the Poles embraced Stanislaus like no other.

Here in Pittsburgh, his spiritual progeny first emigrated to Allegheny City, worshiping at Saint Wenceslas, a close fit as a Bohemian parish. Also living in Birmingham, they attended Saint Michael, a German ethnic parish. Finally, in 1873, some 200 Polish families formed the Saint Stanislaus Beneficial Society both to preserve Polish customs and to form a Polish ethnic parish.

Two years later, in November, 1875, they bought a former Presbyterian church at Penn Avenue and 15th Street, re-casting it as Saint Stanislaus Kostka Church, Pittsburgh's first ethnic Polish Catholic Church. A dozen years later, they sold the original building and replaced it with a church, school, and rectory at 22nd and Smallman Streets. Four years later, in 1891, as school enrollment had ballooned from 300 to 700 students, they expanded once more, to the current site, at the corner of 21st and Smallman Streets.

The Church, typically American mongrel architecture -- Romanesque, Baroque, and Byzantine ruffles and flourishes are visible everywhere -- was consecrated on July 31st, 1892. Today, the bells -- the largest weighs more than a ton; five were electrified in 1956 -- still call people to prayer. While in the old days the pastor preached in Polish, and St. Stan's is still carried on the books as a Polish parish, neither the padre -- for the past four years Father Harry Nichols, who divides his time with nearby St. Patrick's -- nor the people are, in the main, Polish.

These days, Father Nichols lives virtually alone in the 30-room rectory. In its heyday housing four full-time priests and a Holy Family convent, "it was very active," he shrugs. "In the 1960s, it died."

That is not mere hyperbole. In the '60s there was talk of transforming the church into a post office. However, the story goes, Cardinal – then Bishop -- Wright, a man of immense political power, simply put his foot down, and the idea died.

A staunch survivor, St. Stan's seats upwards of 750, including the balcony, which they rarely use these days. Seventy years ago, Father Nichols says, you couldn't get a seat. Now, for his entire weekend slate of masses, *L'église Polonaise* may see 750 total, times certainly having changed.

Still, St. Stan's draws 'em – workers, weekend Strip District shoppers, wanderers from as far as Europe and Asia who come for the church's old-world aura and finely crafted Munich stained glass windows. Fabricated in Germany at the Royal Bavarian Art Institute for $27,672 -- a major expenditure for that time, a cool million in current dollars. While there are many standard themes and images in the glass -- the Holy Mother, Four Gospels, and so on -- particular to this church is the preternaturally young Saint Stanislaus Kostka, surrounded by angels, entering Heaven.

That window, and other artifacts, are part of the rich history pervading the place. Until 1958, when the school was closed, the Holy Family Sisters taught at St. Stan's. And they had good bloodlines: the Mother Foundress, Frances Siedliska herself, brought over the order. "She's now a Blessed," one long-time parishioner proudly says, the Mother, like their own families, making the arduous journey from Poland to America, enduring hard work, extreme privations, abysmal conditions, all while remaining intensely loyal to her faith, language, and heritage.

A last piece of history: on September 20, 1969, John Paul II – then Cardinal Karol Wojtyla -- visited St. Stan's. Remarking how beautiful he found the building, and how much it reminded him of his native Poland, the Cardinal knelt and prayed at a side altar -- where today a small statue marks the spot.

There is no neighborhood around St Stan's any longer, of course, people having moved out of the Strip decades ago. Still, Father Nichols continues to celebrate a daily mass, a pair on Sundays, the original parishioners, or their descendants, returning, from Lawrenceville, from the North and South Hills, where urban migrations have taken them.

"Families come here," he says. "They like the area. They like the church."

CHAPTER THIRTY

ST. MARY OF THE MOUNT CHURCH

Like Peter himself, they built their church upon a rock, this one an enormous sandstone knob high atop Coal Hill, as Mount Washington was known before the American centennial. Towering over Grandview Avenue, the church stands as the Three Rivers' highest house of worship, rising some 400 feet above the Monongahela River.

Taking their motto from *Matthew* (5:14), they proudly proclaim, "You are the light of the world. A city set on a mountain cannot be hidden."

Not hardly. Not St. Mary of the Mount, on a clear day a landmark -- some would call it a beacon -- visible for 50 miles.

Originally part of a 716-acre farm owned by the Penns, the promontory began to take on significance in 1753, when a young George Washington used it to survey the Point. Then, during the Revolution, a British soldier discovered coal on the site -- and the area changed forever. As mines honeycombed what quickly became Coal Hill, coal fires burned in Fort Pitt, shortly thereafter heating the growing city beyond.

After Independence, in 1794 Major Abraham Kirkpatrick -- Revolutionary War veteran, Allegheny County justice of the peace, and Western Army commissary general during the Whiskey Rebellion (who had part of his holdings torched for his pains) -- plunked down 568 pounds, four shillings, and four pence to acquire it.

There the land remained, mined and farmed and relatively unpopulated, until in 1870 the Monongahela Incline, Pittsburgh's first funicular railway, brought easy access to what would shortly be called Mount Washington. After a year, when Mount Washington' population had swelled to some 2,200 people, St. Malachy's, sitting on the South Side below, established a mission in the growing neighborhood. (That need only increased in 1876, when the Monongahela Incline greeted its baby sister funicular, the Duquesne Incline, and people from Duquesne Heights began walking over for church.)

By 1873, it was clear that the people on Mount Washington needed a new building of their own. Assembling two lots at the bend where Belonda Street becomes Kearsarge, they constructed their own chapel. Four years later, the church was named St. Mary of the Mount, officially separating it from St. Malachy's.

Over the next 15 years, the congregation outgrew its intimate, back-street chapel. In April, 1891, Father John O'Connell came to St. Mary's as pastor. A visionary man, and strong leader, he moved St. Mary's -- not to another backstreet neighborhood site, but instead to Grandview Avenue itself. Purchasing a sizeable plot at the corner

of Ulysses Street, he raised some $70,000 to create his stunning neo-Gothic church. With the cornerstone laid within a year of Father O'Connell's arrival, the completed church was dedicated on Sunday, December 19, 1897.

Inside, St. Mary's highly ornate neo-Gothic altar is complimented on both sides by 10 stained glass windows offering a rare pictorial view Christ's life, the private, youthful side as well as the public, adult side. First, as worshippers enter, above them a large stained glass window depicts Christ's Ascension into Heaven. Along the walls they see Christ's life presented from His infancy to His ministry. Here are the Magi; there is the Sermon on the Mount. Here, a gentle Christ welcomes the children; there, a decidedly stern Christ defends the woman taken in adultery. Throughout, the blue-hued windows are figured with great psychological realism and scrupulous attention to detail. (Best supporting actor: a meticulously rendered, appallingly arrogant Pilate.)

As the parish continued to grow in the early years of the 20th Century, St. Mary of the Mount grew with it. After ground was broken in 1909 for a two-story brick school building, the marble halls and stairways rendering it fireproof, the following January 23, while dedicating the newly finished school, Bishop Canevin gave a powerful public address about the necessity of a good Catholic education. So stirring were the Bishop's words, and so pious the congregation, that, while administrators expected 400 students the next day, 635 showed up, many without any previous parochial education.

With the post-World War II boom, the parish again grew, even opening its own high school in 1956. (As Pittsburgh's fortunes waned in the 1980s, so did those of St. Mary of the Mount. Declining enrollment forced the high school's 1982 closing.)

After a full century of service, St. Mary of the Mount presented a new face to Pittsburgh. Not only has there been much touch-up work -- new carpeting and paint have gussied up the old girl -- but in 1999 they constructed a new Bell Tower complete with the latest electronic carillons.

"Every house of worship has a great history," comments Father Michael Stumpf, the current Pastor. "Here, we've seen a lot of change and transformation."

Still, aside from the parish it serves, St. Mary of the Mount maintains a singular hold on Pittsburgh. "What makes this place," Father Stumpf says, "is location, location, location. In *Isaiah* it says, 'people will stream toward this mountain.' Of course, he meant Jerusalem. Here, we take it to mean Mount Washington."

As Pittsburgh's single must-see tourist attraction, one of the rare spots in the world in which a person can stand in the city and look down on the city, out-of-town Catholics stop by for mass -- or a bit of private devotion. "We always have visitors," Father Stumpf says, "hundreds on a good weekend." As such, half the church's

regular draw is from all around the country -- and from such far-flung places as Italy, Thailand, and Nova Scotia. Inevitably moved by St. Mary's beauty, typical is the comment written by one man from Hong Kong. "Thank you," he wrote, "for your beautiful church."

Then there are the less fortunate, those battered souls who use St. Mary's 24-hour, glassed-in vestibule to come in from the cold. Seeking shelter, solace, a spiritual breather before returning to the demons that inhabit the world, both without and within, they write their names, prayers, and pleas for help in the guest book. Suffering the slow burn of loss, the execrable hell of addiction, their scrawled messages are as pitiful as they are moving.

"It's profound what people will write in here," Father Stumpf says.

Perhaps, though, their emotions are only a reflection of what they see. High on the church's altar stand Christ, Mary, and John. On one side, the Sacred Heart of Jesus is pierced with the Crown of Thorns. On the other, the Immaculate Heart of Mary is displayed just prior to the sword stabbing it. These icons, Father Stumpf says, speak to love, struggle, and pain -- states of being well known by those who frequent the church in its oddest hours, in the middle of the night, unseen and unknown.

"Our slogan," Pastor Stumpf says, "is 'keeping spiritual watch over Pittsburgh.' Here," he gestures, "some need it more than others."

CHAPTER THIRTY-ONE

First United Methodist Church

Its genesis came about through begatting of biblical proportions, beginning in 1796 when John Wrenshall, English immigrant, prosperous merchant, and lay preacher arrived in Pittsburgh. Establishing the first Methodist Society and opening a meeting house in the shadow of Fort Pitt, he welcomed soldiers who marched to meetings accompanied by fife and drums -- until the Presbyterians padlocked the place, protesting the assorted heresies of the "free willer."

Undaunted, for the next six years Wrenshall continued his ministry in Fort Pitt itself, then in 1802 moved it into his own home. By 1808 the growing congregation adopted the name Methodist Episcopal Church. Two years later, the church elders bought a lot at Smithfield and Front Streets, near the Monongahela River, and built Pittsburgh's first Methodist church. Integrated from the outset, within two years membership had swelled to 147 white people and 21 African-Americans. Then came a solid century, and more, of moves, schisms, fires, and mergers. For a time, for example, they were at Smithfield Street and Seventh Avenue, but in 1831 a split and a sale brought two buildings, one along what later became Cherry Way, which Macy's still occupies. In 1892, when it was time to leave the 60-year-old church known as the Old Home, H.J. Heinz himself headed the relocation committee, selling the land to the Kaufmann Brothers.

While the church attracted some of the most successful merchants of the day, and espoused what was then a highly radical agenda -- pro-abolition, pro-temperance, pro-women's suffrage -- nothing, it seemed, could stem the tide of factionalism. Finally, in 1891, when the Gothic-style church at Penn and Eighth was lost in a fire, the church splintered again, half crossing the river to Allegheny, half moving to Shadyside, where it remains today.

Of course, there were aftershocks, but, writ small, over 200-plus years some 18 individual churches went into the making of the current First United Methodist Church, at Shadyside's grand intersection of Liberty, Aiken, Centre, and Baum.

They were a wealthy congregation -- in the aggregate, perhaps the wealthiest in the city -- and not afraid to show it. Selling fundraising subscriptions at $100 apiece, it was the kind of group that could wipe out a $30,000 debt in a single night. At a time when steelworkers made two dollars a day, weekly expenses for an average household ran to 16 dollars, and a substantial house in tony Bloomfield or East Liberty cost two-three thousand dollars, the First United Methodist Church cost some $275,000. "It is scarcely surpassed as a triumph of architecture by any Protestant church in this country," one contemporary review crowed.

What did they get for their money? At the time, the country's top architect was Henry Hobson Richardson -- who had already designed Emmanuel Episcopal Church in Allegheny. Because they couldn't hire Richardson himself (the Master had committed the great, unpardonable sin of having passed away in 1888), they would have the nest best thing -- something in his style, a great piece of Romanesque copy work impossible to differentiate from an original.

Completed in 1895, it employed state-of-the-art steel beam support, allowing for some of the largest unsupported interior arches of the time. Using 25,000 cubic feet of stone, one million bricks, 100 tons of iron and steel, and 250,000 feet of lumber, it stood as a construction as well as an aesthetic marvel.

On the mottled sandstone exterior (there is only so much 1950s-era sandblasting and latter-day baking soda baths can do to clean off decades of soft coal soot) there are vines carved all about the building, the inspiration coming from scripture. "I am the vine," *John* 15:5 states, "you are the branches. Those who abide in me, and I in them, bear much fruit."

Inside, its centerpiece is the 800-seat sanctuary under a 140-feet high lantern ceiling, the dome arches four feet larger than Richardson's famous Boston Trinity Church. Inexplicably, a planned chandelier -- which would have illuminated the 100-feet transepts -- was never built, although the church's own electric power plant, and 50 horsepower engine, were.

Dominating the grand space are three enormous stained glass windows. Designed by Tiffany's Edward Sperry, they're dark, brooding, and highly representational – the Sermon on the Mount (which, as at Calvary United Methodist Church, was donated by members of the Horne family, the Apostles enjoined to preach the gospel, and the

marriage at Cana, where water was transformed into wine. The remainder of the stained glass windows, on the walls and in the dome, are various angels, figured in brilliant olive and gold, designed by Boston's Ford & Brooks. Originally, gold-leaf friezes adorned the arches as well, but over the years they were painted over.

"It's a treasure," acknowledges Fred Watts, an architect and chair of the building committee. However, he adds, "it certainly is a responsibility to maintain the church in a way that is respectful of its heritage." When the sanctuary carpet wore out after a century of use, for example, they replicated it -- exactly. "We used a computer," Watts confides.

Similarly, in every case possible they've kept the original pew coverings -- complete with the original cotton stuffing. One thing they couldn't replace was the original light fixtures, now gone from the sanctuary. "As near as I can figure, these escutcheons" -- Watts gestures high on the wall all about the dome's early ascent -- "were Edison lights." Care costs, but First United Methodist has been up to the task. When, for example, the dome needed to be reinforced with steel trusses, they came up with the cool quarter-mil to get the job done right. And when they re-tiled the roof, they bought the same Spanish tile from the same Akron, Ohio manufacturer which had fabricated it more than a century ago. "We try our best to keep it in the original style," Watts acknowledges.

As in many houses of worship, First United Methodist has a chapel, originally designed for smaller, more intimate devotions, now employed to include whole new congregations that the founding merchant princes -- doughty, decorous, addicted to decorum -- would be surprised, if not mightily amused -- to see in their grand Shadyside house of worship. In the chapel, people standing in the need of prayer, whose search for the spiritual is not necessarily expressed in a staid Sunday service, replete with homiletic sermons and hymnal singing, might instead attend a Wednesday night drum circle, slapping a dozen or so skins of various shapes and sizes, textures and timbres.

Although they've wisely retained the Charles Connick-Heinz Chapel-style stained glass windows -- representational scenes all washed in a sea of deep blue -- with the chapel's pews removed, and the moved into a corner, the room seems a bit scattered, like an unkempt playroom. "This gives us more flexibility for different styles of worship," Watts gestures, adding that it hosts everything from weddings to encounter groups. "This room has made some transitions," he smiles wryly. "Everything's kind of shifted around, made much more informal."

CHAPTER THIRTY-TWO

CONGREGATION POALE ZEDECK

It is a grand building, in the Moorish Revival style. A knock-off, really, of the great work of Henry Hornbostel, the architect who left such a powerful legacy across the Pittsburgh landscape -- notably at Rodef Sholom Temple on Fifth Avenue.
Stunning on a smaller scale than its older brother, Congregation Poale Zedeck has interior arches, a glorious blue dome, and delightful terra cotta friezes -- all very much in keeping with religious architecture of the 1920s. (The money was raised, and building dedicated, just before the onset of the Great Depression, which likely would have cancelled the project.) It has soaring stained glass windows -- a breath-taking sunburst, the split-fingered priestly blessing (which Leonard Nimoy adopted for *Star Trek*'s Vulcan "live long and prosper"). It has outsized Lions of Judah protecting the richly wooded Ark of the Covenant.
Yet at Poale Zedeck's heart lies an enigma -- and a tragic story.
Founded in 1881 -- a time when synagogues were separated not only by religiosity but also by ethnicity -- by 40 Orthodox Jewish Austro-Hungarian immigrants, Congregation Poale Zedeck (literally Workers of Righteousness) first used a rented home on a second floor, corner of Grant Street and Second Avenue, Downtown. Keeping pace with the ebb and flow of Jewish neighborhood life as it shifted across the city, in 1885 Poale Zedeck moved to Federal Street (renamed Fernando Street after the 1909 Pittsburgh-Allegheny merger) in the heavily Jewish Hill District. Using those quarters as both synagogue and school,  Poale Zedeck quickly outgrew that space as well, and in 1890 took rooms at Crawford and Rose Streets.
One of two dozen Hill District synagogues, as waves of immigration swelled Pittsburgh's Jewish population, Poale Zedeck thrived for three dozen years on Crawford Street. Yet by the mid-1920s, it was once again time to move, to follow the Jewish migration east, to burgeoning Squirrel Hill. In 1926, the congregation acquired its signature plot at Shady and Philips Avenues. Three years later, they dedicated the building, which, after 80 years, still stands.
"They don't build synagogues like this anymore," comments Adam Reinherz, who married into a four-generation Poale Zedeck family and is writing a history of the building and its people. "It's so ornate, so detailed -- so reminiscent of a classic

European synagogue. Yet," he adds, "there was nothing special about the men who built it. The original founders were tradesmen, honest, hard-working people, good people, who were committed to their synagogue. Putting up this building was their commitment to self-respect. It was one of the duties of membership.

"These men also had a sense of dignity," Reinherz says, "a sense of pride in Poale Zedeck. They built a building to last 100 years -- and in creating something that would last way beyond their years, they envisioned posterity. It was their gift for generations to come."

Yet these tradesmen didn't do it alone -- buildings as grand as Poale Zedeck do not build themselves, nor do they come about by committee. Generally, there is one charmed, charismatic leader who takes charge of the project, raises the funds, sees to all the details.

So it was with Poale Zedeck. For its first four decades, Poale Zedeck grew in its own peripatetic way, led by laymen and visiting rabbis. Finally, with the Great War behind them, and a firm foothold in America, the congregation sought a full-time, permanent rabbi to lead them. Turning to New York City, they discovered an extraordinary man, Rabbi Betzalel Friedman. Coming in 1920, Rabbi Friedman -- whose first name, Betzalel, comes from the Biblical figure who was given the task of creating the Tabernacle -- arrived with glittering credentials. A gifted speaker and Torah scholar, he not only had a law degree from Columbia University, but was also a member of the first graduating class at RIETS – the new Rabbi Yitzchok Elchonon Theological Seminary,

then as now Yeshiva University's advanced program that produces some of the world's leading Orthodox rabbis.

Akin to his Biblical counterpart, Rabbi Friedman was also a builder, a man who united his congregation for a single purpose, to move out of the Hill and into Squirrel Hill, to create its own signature structure -- the single finest in the neighborhood at the time.

Yet by all accounts -- and they are scant, indeed -- Rabbi Friedman had a flinty personality, rubbing the wrong people the wrong way at precisely the wrong time. In an ethnically divided era, he was the wrong ethnicity – Rabbi Friedman was not Hungarian, which in those days mattered. And while Rabbi Friedman steadfastly envisioned a more committed Jewish future, his members wanted to be confirmed in their piety and practice, rather than be prodded to do more.

So he won the battle -- Rabbi Friedman moved his congregation, housing it in Squirrel Hill's premier Orthodox Jewish synagogue, one both traditional and modern, with stained glass walls that are simply priceless today.

His building spoke volumes. As a deliberate copy -- the kind among us would say *homage* -- of Hornbostel, it said, fine, the older, more settled, wealthier German Jews could have big their big Fifth Avenue temple. But so could we, the newer, less wealthy Hungarian Jews. Not on Fifth Avenue, perhaps – that wasn't the way it was done in Eastern Europe. Synagogues were never on Main Street or Market Square. Instead, they were always on side streets, clearly presented, but out of public view. In addition, at Rodef Sholom Hornbostel had his skylight; here at Poale Zedeck we have a central chandelier – if not to rival the Paris Opera House, at least large and prominent, in the Hungarian style, hanging from the Moorish blue dome.

But all this majesty came with a devastating price.

There is much about Rabbi Friedman that we simply don't know – because every vestige of him has been erased. Given the nature of institutional politics, he must have worked tirelessly, raising funds, working with architects, enduring endless meetings, making enemies. In the end, losing the war, he quit -- resigned is a more polite way to put it -- in 1932, a scant three years after he dedicated his masterpiece.

Today, Rabbi Betzalel Friedman is neither revered nor remembered. In a building that, in the manner of many houses of worship, is rife with plaques honoring both donors and the departed, there is not one solitary reference to Rabbi Friedman and his

extraordinary efforts to create the building. It's a true Pyrrhic victory: Poale Zedeck is his building as much as anyone's – and his name appears nowhere in it.

Today, there is virtually no one alive who remembers him. No one speaks of him and his wondrous achievement. He is a wraith in his own monument.

Even the walls are silent.

CHAPTER THIRTY-THREE

SMITHFIELD UNITED CHURCH OF CHRIST

"Well," the dowager huffed one bright Sunday morning, after the Reverend Douglas Patterson had given an interview to a decidedly alternative publication about his decidedly alternative congregation, "this used to be such a *respectable* church!"

"I was very proud of that," he smiles at the memory.

These days, nothing speaks more about the peripatetic history of the Smithfield United Church of Christ more than Doug Patterson. Easy, gentle, expansive of spirit, he epitomizes the church militant as it is today -- a far cry from *volks kirche* it once was.

"In 12 years," he adds, "the face of the congregation has changed dramatically. Now, we have families. We have children. We have young people. We have gays and lesbians. We've worked hard to solidify as the United Church of Christ -- and become a very diverse, inclusive congregation.

"We've always had a congregational heritage," Patterson adds. "We trace our heritage back to the Puritans. Fiercely independent."

That lineage may come as something of a surprise to the Germans who organized, populated, and funded the church for nearly two centuries. (German was dropped as the official language only in 1928 -- when it became increasingly difficult to draft German-speaking clergy from *das alte land*. However, even recently, when they tried to take "*Stille Nacht*" off the Christmas Eve program, they faced the wrath of die-hard traditionalists.) In fact, it's been a long, circuitous path from those sober, straight-laced German Protestants to the polyglot congregation they boast today.

Time, for Smithfield United, starts in 1782; so for the church's 225th anniversary, in 2007, they issued a statement calling themselves "Pittsburgh's oldest original congregation."

"We got *scathing* letters," Patterson smiles. "It was interesting."

Of course, other denominations claim bragging rights -- there were local church services decades prior to their 1782 start date -- but, Patterson counters, "this is the oldest official *organized* church."

Be that as it may, or may not, the Smithfield congregation was indeed founded in 1782, when Pittsburgh already had a solid German presence. When 42 men -- including Lutherans, Reformed, and unaffiliateds -- signed their names on the membership roll, they established a church that embraced a wealth of conviction.

Renting a log cabin, they called east for a minister, Reverend Johann Wilhelm Weber, who traversed the Allegheny Mountains on horseback. The following year, 1783, the congregation built a one-room log meeting house at Diamond Alley (now Forbes Avenue) and Wood Street.

A mere four years later, the John Penns, *père et fils*, deeded the congregation God's little half-acre on Smithfield Street. Erecting a building four years after that, in 1791, in 1812 a second group joined the first and the newly merged congregation re-branded itself the German Evangelical Protestant Church.

As the congregation grew, they built three more churches, 1815, 1833 (where Henry John Heinz, founder of the famous food dynasty, was baptized in 1844), and 1875. Various mergers and schisms followed, including a split with the Lutherans, who, wanting to switch to English, moved up to Grant Street.

By the time the Twenties roared, they were ready for a new home, the cornerstone ceremony for the current building attracting an overflow crowd in 1926. Built by Pastor Carl Voss, who served 1905-43, he specified that the main sanctuary be on the second floor -- an oddity -- thereby moving services away from the noise of the streetcars rumbling down Smithfield Street. As the fifth church on Smithfield -- and sixth location overall -- it is another Henry Hornbostel masterpiece, marked by its strong Gothic lines, poured plaster ornamental ceiling, 80-foot steel-and-aluminum spire (the world's first use of architectural aluminum), and Pittsburgh historical stained glass windows.

Fabricated by the Von Gerichten studios of Columbus, the windows are surprisingly subtle and muted. While the top half depicts the life of Jesus, the bottom presents selected moments in Pittsburgh history:

President-elect Abraham Lincoln visiting Pittsburgh on the way to his first inauguration, 1861. (He was here a second time, too, four long, war-torn years later, as his funeral train passed through.)

George Washington and Friedrich Von Steuben, 1778. Neither a general nor a *Von* in the Old Country, it took a bit of chicanery and sell to net him a Continental Army commission. His first tour of duty: Valley Forge.

Smithfield's first pastor, Johann Wilhelm Weber, crossing the Allegheny Mountains on horseback, 1782. He rode for a solid month to get here.

The John Penns, elder and younger, signing over the land, 1787. (Leasing the rest of the block -- Centre City Tower to Brooks Brothers -- has meant financial solvency for the church.)

The Fort Pitt Blockhouse, 1764, which served as an early meeting house for Pittsburgh Methodists.

The Point, 1817, based on a famous sketch by Mrs. E.C. Gibson on her honeymoon.

Smithfield Street Bridges, 1860, showing the city's first wooden bridge, 1818-45, lost in the Great Fire, and John Roebling's 1846 replacement, his first wire-rope suspension bridge, which in turn was followed by Gustav Lindenthal's 1883 lenticular bridge, still standing.

Their own early churches, 1791-1814, 1815-1832, 1833-1875.

Their previous grand church, 1875-1924.

Pittsburgh's Court House and Market House, 1825.

"These windows," Patterson gestures, "are in line with the thinking of this church over the years. Open, progressive, demanding that our members pursue truth in all different ways -- including science and philosophy."

Happily ensconced in its new home, in 1968 the Smithfield Congregational Church brought in the neighboring Smithfield Methodist Brimstone Church, razing the latter to make way for Centre City Tower.

Apparently, though, the new Smithfield United Church ignored their own Gospel, in *Matthew* and *Luke*, that one cannot serve two masters. Federated but confused, the merger meant two sets of everything -- essentially meaning one set of nothing. By 1994, the congregation had to choose, or risk going under; the Congregationalists stayed.

Although Smithfield United certainly show signs of health, in the old days the church drew 800 at a clip; now, they barely break the century mark. In the old days, Patterson says, "we had people who could write big checks. We don't have that anymore." He pauses and smiles. "It's OK.

"Now, my parishioners come from all over the place," he adds, from as far as Cranberry and Little Washington. "I have a corporate church. It's not an urban church. It's not an inner-city church. It's a Downtown church. And when people come Downtown to a Downtown church they have higher expectations."

Not only the breath-taking beauty of the space, but also the quality of the worship services. "We put a lot of effort into it," he says. "Our music is superb." Not only the organ, which is a given, but also such guests as retired Pittsburgh Symphony concert master Andrés Cárdenes, with whom Patterson played a guitar-violin "Amazing Grace" duet one Sunday morning. Having preached on Taking Risks, he figured *why not*? and reached for his guitar. Totally unrehearsed, the two launched into the splendid old hymn. "I was sweating bullets," Patterson admits.

From all accounts, he, and the maestro, did just fine.

CHAPTER THIRTY-FOUR

St. Augustine Church

Sunday, September 14, 2008, was full of scudding skies and high winds -- winds so strong that they brought Saint Augustine's century-old copper cross crashing down on the church's steps, shattering the metal, chewing up the concrete. "It was a pretty bad storm," Father John Daya recalls of the day, the Feast of the Exaltation of the Holy Cross. "It was ferocious." He pauses. "It was a miracle that no one was hurt."

From the first, Saint Augustine has been that way -- a church of miracles, or, for the more secular-minded, odd coincidences.

Time begins in 1860. A sleepy industrial suburb, Lawrenceville, named for War of 1812 naval hero James "Don't give up the ship!" Lawrence, boasted the arsenal (blown to Kingdom Come two years later), some 70 new houses, and a freshly paved Butler Street. However, in terms of village history, the year's big event was a meeting.

With the critical mass of Catholic children needing a bigger school, village elders decided it was time to add their own church -- a German Catholic church. Helped by the new Society of German Catholics of Lawrenceville, Father George Kircher organized the parish. Within a year, they had drawn up plans for a 100-foot-long, 650-seat church with a 150-foot-high tower.

As parish families were contributing 10 cents monthly for the building, it was decided to name the church for Saint Augustine -- not necessarily out of a special devotion to the Church Father, but instead to honor Augustine Hoeveler, a generous patron and influential lay leader. Between the donor and the dimes, by 1862 the parish had the $12,000 needed to build the first church, whose facade is still visible on 37th Street, halfway down the block from the current church.

Laying the cornerstone on June 22, 1862, finishing the roof the following December, religious orders from around the city marched to the Romanesque red brick building on Thanksgiving, 1863, to hear Bishop Michael Domenec bless the new church.

A decade later, 1873, St. Augustine enjoyed a seemingly odd, but ultimately fruitful marriage. As the fiercely anti-Catholic Otto von Bismarck was busy running the Franciscan-Capuchins out of Bavaria, Bishop Domenec invited them to Pittsburgh to staff St. Augustine Church, German-speaking friars for a German-speaking parish.

The sea change came on April 19, 1874, when Father Hyacinth Epp became St. Augustine's pastor and added Capuchin devotions. The happy recipient of enormous industrial growth in Pittsburgh, Father Epp worked to keep pace with his parish's unprecedented expansion. In addition to newly arriving industrial families, hundreds of others came from the Strip, forced to relocate by the construction of the Pennsylvania

Railroad's Union Station. As such, in 1874 the church added a 100-foot transept, 350 seats, and an ornately carved altar, pulpit, and communion rail. The result, many thought, was one of the finest churches in Pittsburgh.

When insurrection came to Lawrenceville, Father Maurice Greck, Saint Augustine's second Capuchin pastor and a former military officer, was ready to handle it. In July, 1877, striking railroad workers rioted in Lawrenceville. As the battle raged back and forth, one of the soldiers was wounded in front of St. Augustine Church. Taking him through the church into the adjacent monastery, the friars administered first aid -- while the rioters tried to force their way into the monastery to capture the soldier. Not on Father Greck's watch! Standing in the doorway, refusing to let the rioters in the building, he used his best military voice and ordered them off church grounds. Unwilling to attack the priest, they skulked away -- and the soldier's life was spared.

Adding a school, rectory, and monastery, by the late 1890s St. Augustine seemed fit for the new century -- except that the 40-year-old building needed extensive repairs.

Matters came to a head when Pastor Charles Speckert asked Mrs. Mary Regina Frauenheim, and her daughter Rose, for a substantial contribution. *Sponsor some new, beautiful windows, perhaps*? Father Speckert asked.

Balking, the ladies Frauenheim retorted that such an aged and infirm building wasn't worth new, beautiful windows.

Shrugging, Father Speckert said that if they were willing to donate, say, $50,000, then he would build them a new beautiful church.

While the Father may have been joking -- parish debt alone stood at $30,000 -- the Frauenheims took him seriously. Asking for time to think, a few days later Aloysius Frauenheim himself -- owner of Pittsburgh Brewing -- pledged the full amount.

It was an offer that the dumbfounded Father Speckert couldn't refuse. Paying the full amount for the land alone, clearing 16 houses from the corner site, they wondered what church they would build -- until one of the friars saw a picture of Saint Benno Church in Munich, which they immediately adopted as a model.

But when John T. Comes drew up the plans, and the bids came in, the amount seemed impossible: $100,000 for construction.

It's no use, the distraught Father told the Frauenheims.

It's no problem, they responded, and simply doubled their gift.

Some 5,000 people attended the 1899 cornerstone laying, and the entire parish seemed to watch as the church ascended brick by brick, the dome rising 92 feet, the twin towers 56 feet higher, "twin arms raised in prayer," one man wrote, "over Lawrenceville." On

May 12, 1901, a procession from the old church walked over a flower-strewn path to the new building. So popular was the church -- and populous the parish -- that Father Ignatius Weisbruch paid the remaining debt in a mere 11 years.

What they got for their money has remained virtually untouched for a century. Although the congregation has changed along with the neighborhood -- "it's a melting pot, really," Father Daya says, with vestiges of older German, Irish, and Polish communities. And while the church was folded into a larger, more inclusive parish in 1993 -- Our Lady of the Angels Parish merged Saint John the Baptist, Liberty Avenue; Saint Augustine, 37th Street; Saint Mary, 46th Street, and Holy Family, 44th Street -- still, the building is all German all the time.

The German iron cross (*eisernes kreuz*) -- unfortunately adopted by the National

Socialists and other assorted miscreants -- appears over the door and in the marble communion rail. The soaring stained glass windows, all imported from Innsbruck, Austria, have a decided Teutonic cast to the cast -- Ambrose, Albertus Magnus, Gregory, Jerome, all posed in front of architectural filigree work, a classic German touch. "I relate to the whole space," says Father Daya, a nine-year veteran. "Every time I walk into the church, it's breath-taking, captivating. It's a great place for worship."

Great as it is, the building could use a bit of touch-up. Father Daya gestures at his lovely, unique canvas Stations of the Cross, sadly faded by time and heat. They, too, could use a good wash, perm, and set. Alas, the Hoevelers and the Frauenheims are long gone, the neighborhood has changed, and funds are not forthcoming. "I don't have $25,000 to get them restored," he sighs and shakes his head.

CHAPTER THIRTY-FIVE

ST. JOHN CHRYSOSTOM BYZANTINE CATHOLIC CHURCH

He walked holding his mother's hand, a small, sickly child, noticeably talented, with a nose so big his family called him Andy the Red-Nosed Warhola. Together, they'd come from Oakland, along Dawson Street to Swinburne, down Greenfield Avenue, finally to Saline Street, the little boy and his beloved mother, there to listen to the liturgy in foreign tongues, to look up at the icons, to drink in the colors, the majesty, there to forge a vision, and a style.

Talented, inarticulate, inward, he'd spend hours in church, staring up at the outsized, primitive images, Byzantine images, floor to ceiling all about him, folk art of hovering saints, all red and blue, green and brown. Mary with her parents, Joachim and Anne. John the Baptist with his parents, Zachary and Elizabeth. St. John Chrysostom (roughly the Golden-Tongued), patron of the church. St. Nicholas of Myra, patron of Slavic peoples, known for performing miracles and giving gifts to the poor. Morphed over the centuries into Little Saint Nick, lionized by the Beach Boys and countless others, somehow losing two syllables in his name, Nicholas clarifying like butter into Claus, Santa, scourge of chimneys, bringer of all things sweet to children on Christmas Eve.

The nascent Pop Art *meister* must have been overwhelmed by the explosion of almond-eyed figures: the Three Hierarchs -- St. John, St. Basil the Great, Saint Gregory. Prophets, saints, disciples. Christ in the ceiling. In the Holy of Holies, an enormous Mary, the baby Jesus inside her, must have seemed four stories tall, those warm Eastern eyes staring down at him, boring into his soul.

Baptized at St. John Chrysostom Byzantine Catholic Church, Andy Warhol was a regular attendee, 1928-1949, until he left Carnegie Tech, and Pittsburgh, more or less for good. "The church profoundly influenced him," avers Peter Oresick, self-admitted Warhol afflictee, author of *Warhol-o-rama*, and a distant relative, "the iconostasis, or icon screen, the stacked images of saints in the Russian style, floor to ceiling, more than 40 feet high."

These days, though, church regulars laugh, a bit contemptuously, when they mention Warhol, as if he, his fortune and fame, simply don't belong in the world of lower Greenfield, one of working class folks attending a decidedly family church, one given

more than its requisite 15 minutes of fame not for its astounding icons, but instead for an odd duck, a wildly wealthy renegade, who came back only to be buried in their cemetery.

These people stand as the direct descendents of the church's founders, who arrived threadbare and bedraggled in the industrialized 19th Century. Coming from the Carpathians, crossing the Atlantic, then traveling hundreds of miles across an unknown land, they found work and made a new home adjacent to a Jones & Laughlin steel mill. Populating Greenfield, or more precisely Lower Greenfield, or Four Mile Run, or just the Run, or *Rushka Dolina*, Russian Valley, by 1910 they found the trek from the long, low neighborhood to St. John Church on the South Side too arduous. Undertaking to found a new parish in the Run, at first they rented a hall on Saline Street. Purchasing land, that year they built their own frame church, one that would serve as sanctuary and social hall for the next half-century.

Six years later, 1916, the first portion of the icon screen was built. According to the Byzantine rite, such two-dimensional representations are not merely decorations, but actual icons, inspiring contemplation, communication, and prayer. "Endow them with the power to cure sickness," they were blessed at the time of their consecration, "and to dispel the temptations of the devil."

With the church and parish house dedicated October 28, 1917, and the full icon screen dedicated October 12, 1919, as the '20s roared, and the mills ran 24-hour shifts, the congregation outgrew its wooden home. Still on Saline Street, they laid the cornerstone for a new brick church in 1932, the finished product rising in midst of the Great Depression. Hardly a wealthy population -- or neighborhood, for that matter -- the congregation nevertheless persevered. "People were very generous," offers Reverend Thomas Schaefer, the current pastor. Even in hard times, families gave as much as $50 toward the church -- a lot of money in those days.

After the 1935 dedication, St. John Chrysostom, with its domes and Byzantine crosses, became such a landmark off the Parkway East that legend has it that on his 1959 visit to Pittsburgh Soviet Premier Nikita Krushchev -- all five-feet-four of him -- was so taken with the Eastern cut of the church, reminding him of his boyhood home in the coal- and-steel town of Donetsk, Ukraine, that he stopped his motorcade to look at the Slavic church in the Run.

Of course, he saw what everyone else does -- the Byzantine crosses rising adjacent to the roadway. Of course, there are competing explications of the symbolism. In one reading, the top beam represents the plaque bearing the inscription Jesus of Nazareth, King of the Jews, while the slanted bottom beam suggests the scale of justice. Some go a step further, adding that while one of the thieves crucified with Jesus repented his sin,

accepted Jesus as the Messiah, and was thus lifted into heaven, the other thief rejected Jesus and was therefore damned to hell.

What Krushchev didn't see were the steep stairs, the sanctuary on the second floor, meant to parallel the spiritual ascent experienced in church. He also missed the anomalous Romanesque stained glass windows, an odd marriage of Eastern and Roman rites. And he didn't approach the altar in St. John's, split in two parts, deliberately reminiscent of the Holy of Holies in the Temple of Jerusalem.

After some six decades, with the old girl needing a bit of touch-up, in 1994 they began planning a major renovation, including more icons. "The idea in a Byzantine church," Father Schaefer says, "is that everything is covered, that everything is inspiring." The new lighting, too, offers 20 different settings, from clouded and contemplative to bright and blasting, depending on the mass and the mood. Three years later, 1997, they were finished.

Perhaps not quite. For what would any house of worship be without a good unanswered question? In the church's rear there is a decidedly World War II-era window featuring American and Vatican shields, depicting soldiers and sailors, WACS and WAVES, pausing piously by the grave of a fallen comrade. It is a proud patriotic gesture, to be sure, but completely out of character with rest of St. John Chrysostom. Why this window in this place? Father Schaefer shrugs: it's a story lost to the ages.

In those post-war old days, he adds, St. John Chrysostom drew some 500 at a clip, running two or three masses every Sunday. In these more secular times, the solitary Sunday mass pulls 120 -- on a good day. Well, he shrugs, the numbers really don't tell the entire story. Gazing at the grand tattooed interior, he smiles. "This is a pretty amazing church," he says.

CHAPTER THIRTY-SIX

TRINITY CATHEDRAL

Despite all its history, despite predating the Revolution and standing as one of Pittsburgh's great cathedrals, what people most cherish about Trinity Cathedral are little things -- the Boys Choir, for example, and the Cathedral Lunchroom. "This is a place that holds sacred memories," says Canon Catherine Brall, the current pastor. "It's the heart and soul of working folks Downtown."

Begun in 1913, the Boys Choir ran for a good half-century, 48 boys and 12 men paid $2 a month for carfare. Their voices angelic, and silenced when too many members moved too far away, hardly a month passes that Canon Brall doesn't run into a grown and graying man who once sang at Trinity -- and remembers it fondly. "That's one of the really neat things about this church," she smiles.

Another was the Cathedral Lunchroom. Back in the Roaring '20s, when respectable women wouldn't walk in a saloon for lunch, the Trinity Girls Friendly Society opened a lunchroom as a safe haven for working women to eat. Advertised as a place where women could find not only healthy, sanitary meals, but also "recreation and mental renewal," the Lunchroom became a key place for women to get hot lunches at reasonable prices," Canon Brall says. Back in the day, that meant soup, sandwich, and coffee with cream for eight to 15 cents, depending.

Quiet memories, certainly, but part of more than 250 years of history at Trinity Cathedral. Beginning life as an inland oasis, the land was far enough from the Point-area wetlands to serve as a Native American burial ground, sacred earth set apart from the bustle and the battles, the floods and the flotsam near the rivers.

Following suit, the French similarly interred their dead there, as did British colonists and American settlers. While Pittsburgh Anglican worship began at Fort Pitt in 1758, Trinity Cathedral essentially took its first breath in October 1787 when the William Penn heirs gave three lots -- including the graveyard -- to the new American Episcopal and Presbyterian churches. Although the deed does not name Trinity *per se*, the trustees chosen to receive the land were active in Trinity's creation. (For example, John Ormsby was a Fort Pitt lay reader as early as 1762.)

Although the church owned the Sixth Avenue site, for nearly two decades the congregation met in homes and on the second floor of the Market Square courthouse. Finally buying a triangular piece of land at Sixth and Liberty Avenues, they built an octagonal church -- immediately mis-labeled the Round Church. Setting the cornerstone on July 1, 1805, they supervised the Robinson Brothers, Contractors, to erect their small but sturdy home in just 69 days. With 42 pews, a gallery, and a Georgian-style pulpit, the first Trinity was a beautiful little building, dignified and significant, well worth the Robinsons' 56-pound, eight-shilling, nine-pence fee.

As lovely and intimate as it was, within 20 years the church was deemed too small, and in 1824 Trinity built what many consider the first Gothic structure in Pittsburgh. Designed by the rector, John Henry Hopkins, a multi-talented Jeffersonian fellow who tripled as a lawyer and an architect, he moved Trinity to its present site. Brick covered with stucco to look like stone, the second Trinity featured a long chancel with side galleries, a spire, buttresses, arches, and seats for 1,000. A major building in an increasingly important city, it was consecrated by William White, Pennsylvania's first Episcopal bishop, on June 12, 1825.

Standing through 1871, one early indication of its importance in Pittsburgh occurred in 1845. After the April 10 fire destroyed a goodly portion of the city, Trinity distributed food, clothing, and shelter to hundreds of survivors. During the Civil War, as Trinity shipped much-needed supplies south, Felix Brunot himself led the way through Confederate lines.

As a cathedral, it has hosted its share of famous people, including, for example, the baptisms of both Stephen Foster and Mary Cassatt. In February, 1861, Mr. Lincoln stopped by *en route* to his first inauguration.

After the war, Pittsburgh was declared the seat of the Episcopal diocese, and although a bishop was duly appointed, the church was not named a cathedral for another 62 years. Nevertheless, in 1869 it was felt that they needed a bigger -- a grander -- space, and so in June laid the cornerstone. The current Trinity Church was dedicated January 25, 1872.

Combining English Gothic with a Romanesque barrel vault ceiling, Trinity features a 200-foot spire, sandstone columns and piers, hand-carved white butternut, walnut, and mahogany woodwork, and of course stained glass windows.

World War I brought War Bond and Liberty Fund drives, and volunteers rolling bandages, knitting warm clothing, writing letters to soldiers overseas. In 1922, the choir sang for stage star Lillian Russell's funeral -- the same year the new marble pulpit was installed.

When, in 1927, Trinity Church finally became Trinity Cathedral, it required, among other things, that morning and evening prayers be offered daily without exception -- which Trinity has faithfully executed, even during the 1936 St. Patrick's Day Flood, the 1950 Thanksgiving Blizzard, and its own 1967 fire, which destroyed a number of the stained glass windows. When Trinity re-opened, with 1960s-style neo-medieval

windows replacing those lost, the Duke Ellington Orchestra celebrated the occasion. So hot were the sounds that people danced in the aisles, causing something of a scandal -- as did the 1980 invitation to President Jimmy Carter (a Baptist, for Heaven's sake) to make a last-minute, ultimately unsuccessful campaign stop.

Still, Trinity has never allowed the land's original usage to be lost. Calling it Pittsburgh's oldest unreconstructed landmark, its sliver of a cemetery was once an entire city block, containing some 4,000 graves. Carefully removing and reinterring those remains which were unidentifiable, they preserved as many of the original markers as possible. Some are simple slabs, marred and worn by the passing years; others are larger monuments etched in soot from the dark time when mills burned soft coal and

rendered the skies black.

Here, in the crook of the building, lies Red Pole, aka Mio-Qua-Coo-Na-Caw, the Shawnee chief who signed a 1795 treaty bringing peace to the frontier -- and who later died at Fort Pitt, despite the best ministrations of Nathaniel Bedford, the region's first physician.

There, General William and Colonel James Butler, heroes of the Revolution and the Defense of the Republic, 1812, along with Oliver Ormsby, an early Pittsburgh Brahmin for whom Mount Oliver was named, along with daughters Sarah and Jane, who entered the local lexicon as South Side streets.

Here, skilled glassworker William Peter Eichbaum, who toiled in the court of Louis XVI, emigrated to the New World, and lent his anglicized name -- Oak Tree -- to Oakland.

There, Alfred Irenaeus Hopkins, an infant, who lived 1829-30, and William Edward Muller, a 22-year-old bridegroom who left this Earth a scant 20 days shy of his 23rd birthday -- and a week before his nuptials.

The year 1853 saw the last burial here, George Shiras, a Whiskey Rebellion militiaman and father of Charles Shiras, Stephen Foster's lyricist.

"Here," Canon Brall gestures, "we have a reverence for the dead."

Addresses and Locations

1. St. Mary of Mercy, Boulevard of the Allies and Stanwix Street, Downtown
2. Beulah Presbyterian Church, 2500 McCrady Road, Churchill
3. First Presbyterian Church, 320 Sixth Avenue, Downtown
4. Emmanuel Episcopal Church, 957 West North Avenue, North Side
5. Saint John the Baptist Ukrainian Catholic Church, 109 South 7th Street, South Side
6. Immaculate Heart of Mary Church, 3058 Brereton Street, Polish Hill
7. Muslim Community Center of Greater Pittsburgh, 233 Seaman Lane, Monroeville
8. Saint Louise de Marillac Church, 320 McMurray Road, Upper St. Clair
9. First Hungarian Reformed Church of Homestead, 416 East 10th Avenue, PA 15120, Homestead
10. Temple Emanuel of South Hills, 1250 Bower Hill Road, PA 15243, Mount Lebanon
11. Pittsburgh New Church, 299 Le Roi Road Pittsburgh, PA 15208, Point Breeze
12. Sri Venkateswara Temple, 1230 South McCully Drive, PA 15235, Penn Hills
13. Zen Center of Pittsburgh, 124 Willow Ridge Road, PA 15143, Sewickley
14. Old St. Patrick's Church, 1711 Liberty Avenue, Strip District
15. Pittsburgh Sikh Gurdwara, 4407 McKenzie Drive, Monroeville
16. Saint Nicholas of Myra Byzantine Catholic Church, 5400 Tuscarawas Road, PA 15009, Beaver
17. St. Anthony's Chapel, 1704 Harpster Street, PA 15212, Troy Hill
18. St. Nicholas Croatian Catholic Church, 24 Maryland Avenue, PA 15209, Millvale
19. Macedonia Church of Pittsburgh, 2225 Bedford Avenue, PA15219, Hill District
20. St. Nicholas Orthodox Church, 320 Munson Avenue, PA 15136, McKees Rocks
21. Rodef Shalom Congregation, 4905 Fifth Avenue, PA 15213 Oakland
22. St. Paul Cathedral, 108 North Dithridge Street, PA 15213, Oakland
23. East Liberty Presbyterian Church, 116 South Highland Avenue, PA 15206, East Liberty
24. Heinz Memorial Chapel, University of Pittsburgh Campus, South Bellefield Avenue, PA 15260, Oakland
25. Hindu Jain Temple, 615 Illini Drive, PA15146, Monroeville

26. The Presbyterian Church of Sewickley, 414 Grant Street, PA 15143, Sewickley
27. Calvary United Methodist Church, 971 Beech Avenue, PA 15233, North Side
28. St. Benedict the Moor Church, Watt Street (Freedom Corner), PA 15219, Hill District
29. St. Stanislaus Kostka Church, 57 21st Street, PA 15222, The Strip District
30. St Mary of the Mount Church, 403 Grandview Avenue, PA 15211, Mount Washington
31. First United Methodist Church, 5401 Centre Avenue, PA 15232, Shadyside
32. Congregation Poale Zedeck, Shady and Phillips Avenues, PA 15217, Squirrel Hill
33. Smithfield United Church of Christ, 620 Smithfield Street, PA 15222, Downtown
34. Saint Augustine Church, 225 37th Street, PA 15201, Lawrenceville
35. St. John Chrysostom Church, 506 Saline Street, PA 15207
36. Trinity Cathedral, 328 Sixth Avenue, PA 15222, Downtown

Photo Credits

Photographs by Brian Cohen copyright © 2012, except pages 24, 27, 36, 37, 91, 149, 152, copyright © 2012 Tim Fabian.

www.ingramcontent.com/pod-product-compliance
Lightning Source LLC
Chambersburg PA
CBHW041608220426
43667CB00001B/3